ROTHERHAM TROLLEYBUSES

Colin Barker

Series editor Robert J Harley

Front Cover: One of the forty four post war Daimler trolleybuses, namely 5 (originally 9), passes the Dale Road Rawmarsh depot of the Mexborough and Swinton Company as it returns to Rotherham from Adwick Road on the operators' joint service. Some of these vehicles saw further service in Spain after withdrawal, while others received new double deck bodies in 1956/57.
(G Lumb/Travel Lens Photographic)

Rear Cover: This view depicts one of the post war single deck Daimlers after re-bodying into double deck format. The extra seating capacity of the twenty vehicles so treated helped extend the life of the system until its closure in 1965. 36 (originally single deck 92) is seen in Corporation Street destined for Kimberworth (Ewers Road). The power station cooling towers dominate the skyline behind the Turf Tavern public house, which is situated on the corner of Upper Millgate. (Photobus)

This publication is dedicated to two recently deceased bus and trolleybus photographers, whose camera work appears both in this, and my earlier albums.

Roy Marshall died in May after a long illness. He was both an enthusiast photographer and a professional busman, starting his career with Skills of Nottingham, and eventually holding the General Managerships of Galligaer, Burton-on-Trent, and finally Burnley and Pendle.

John Fozard also died in May following a particularly tragic domestic accident. In addition to his photographic activities, he was also a railway modeller.

Their work has provided a visual historical record of the British public transport scene, for which we are indebted.

Published October 2013

ISBN 978 1 908174 49 9

© Middleton Press, 2013

Design Deborah Esher

Published by
    Middleton Press
    Easebourne Lane
    Midhurst
    West Sussex
    GU29 9AZ
Tel: 01730 813169
Fax: 01730 812601
Email: info@middletonpress.co.uk
www.middletonpress.co.uk

Printed in the United Kingdom by Henry Ling Limited, at the Dorset Press, Dorchester, DT1 1HD

CONTENTS

INTRODUCTION
AND ACKNOWLEDGMENTS

When I was preparing the album on the Mexborough and Swinton trolleybus system in this Middleton Press series, I had contemplated combining it with that of Rotherham, given their joint working arrangements, but decided that there was sufficient scope for a publication on each operator.

The Rotherham trolleybus system was one of the first to open in the United Kingdom, and the first to operate outside a borough boundary. It was of interest in operating only single deck vehicles until double deck trolleybuses were used towards the system's end. Some of the former were retained to operate over the joint Mexborough and Swinton routes, which passed under low bridges. A number of the single deckers also finished up with Spanish operators after withdrawal.

This publication is not intended to be a detailed history of the system, but more a pictorial record of the routes that Rotherham's trolleybuses travelled, and the vehicles that were operated. Whilst the content will be of interest to the transport enthusiast, it should provide material for those interested in the social history of the area.

Enthusiasts, copyright holders and archive organisations, have provided the photographs; my thanks go to them for their generosity. Due accreditation has been given with each view, but there are a few where I have been unable to establish the source; I hope the originators feel their work has enhanced the publication. The arrangement of photographs starts from the town centre, and then follows each route from date of introduction along the main arteries.

Having never seen the system in operation, I have been heavily dependent on fellow enthusiasts, and my thanks go to Paul Fox, Mike Johnson, Laurie Johnson and David Careless (the latter living in Canada) for their response to my many questions and queries, plus agreeing to read through the first draft.

Roger Smith prepared the map, Terry Russell the line drawings, Eric Old provided the tickets, and Philip and Dorothy Crutchley identified a number of photograph locations following a chance holiday meeting. My thanks go to all of the above.

Finally thanks go to my wife Maureen, who has supported me with this project, accompanying me on research visits to South Yorkshire, and once again using her computer skills to provide the publisher with a usable format.

For a more comprehensive history of the Rotherham operation readers are referred to the following: -

British Bus and Tram Systems *No 33 by Charles C Hall*

Buses Illustrated *Nos 80/81 (1961/62)*

Rotherham and District Transport *by Charles C Hall*
Volumes 1,2 and 3 ISBN 0 90366 89 8, 92 8 and 93 6

HISTORICAL AND GEOGRAPHICAL BACKGROUND

Rotherham is situated at the confluence of the Rivers Rother and Don in South Yorkshire, with Sheffield 5.5 miles (8.8 km) to the south west. The boundary between the two towns was at Tinsley, with the current M1 motorway dissecting the two urban conurbations. The area is hilly, with steep inclines on the Kimberworth and Thrybergh services.

The main north to south stage coach routes, and initial railway lines, passed by Rotherham, but the town established a presence when the North Midland line opened between Derby and Leeds in 1840, the local Sheffield to Rotherham service having commenced in 1838.

The area around Rotherham was mentioned in the Domesday Book, and there were settlements during the Iron Age, plus the Roman Occupation, the latter establishing a camp at Templeborough. Rotherham established itself as a key Saxon town near a favourable river crossing.

In the 1480s, the Archbishop of York, Thomas Rotherham, instigated the building of a college, which was to rival those of Oxford and Cambridge. However it was dissolved in the 1540s during the reign of Edward VI. The college, plus the building of All Saints' Parish Church, made Rotherham a fashionable and modern town by the beginning of the 16th century. By the beginning of the next century its reputation had deteriorated.

Although the area had been exploited for iron since Roman times, it was to be the discovery of coal that triggered the town towards industrialisation. This led to the River Don being made navigable by 1740, as the iron and steel industries grew in the late 18th and early 19th centuries, the latter continuing as a major employer, until the decline in the late 20th century.

The first glass works was opened in the mid-18th century, and this industry still continues. In the 19th century, other industries developed including pottery and brass manufacture. During this time local canals were built to carry incoming materials, and to transport finished goods and coal out of the area; however the railways eventually overtook the majority of these. Flour production was another important industry, which continued to as late as 2008.

The rapid growth that came with the industrial development is illustrated by the fact that the population of Rotherham in 1801 was 17,191, which had grown to 119,915 by 1901. This led to the need for some form of public transport, particularly between the town and the bottom of Rawmarsh Hill.

Manufacturing has declined in the recent past, with the closure of coal mines and steel factories. Some steel production has continued in the area, although on a much reduced scale, with the main focus on the production of specialist products. This decline in coal and manufacturing activity saw the start of an urban re-generation project in 2007 known as "Rotherham Renaissance".

PUBLIC TRANSPORT HISTORY

The earliest proposals for a horse tramway resulted from the heavy carrier traffic between Rotherham and Parkgate (at the bottom of Rawmarsh Hill). A number of schemes were considered, the earliest in the 1870s, but all were withdrawn, or where powers had been granted, they were allowed to lapse.

The first indication that the Corporation was considering trams came in 1898, and in the following year both Rotherham and Rawmarsh deposited Bills to build electric tramways; Royal Assent was given to both in 1900. The Rawmarsh Bill was taken over by the Mexborough and Swinton Tramway Company, with territory to the north of Rotherham, and included plans for the two operators to run over each other's systems.

In Rotherham, the tram system commenced on the 31st January 1903, and routes were opened progressively to Kimberworth, Canklow, Dalton/Thrybergh, Templeborough/Tinsley and Broom Road. Tinsley was on the road to Sheffield, who also operated a service to this location. For a number of years the two termini were separate, but eventually in September 1905 through joint working was instigated between the two towns.

Second hand cars were purchased during the 1914-1918 War, plus new vehicles in the 1920s. However, trolleybuses were beginning to make their mark, and had gradually replaced trams on most routes by the mid 1930s. One exception was the joint tram service to Sheffield, with Rotherham purchasing a batch of single ended cars in 1934/5, together with the refurbishment of some earlier vehicles. This service continued throughout the 1939-1945 War, and the last tram ran on 12th November 1949.

Although in the opening years the Council were happy with their tramway, and were considering extensions into the surrounding areas, as early as 1903 the Electrical Engineer was asked to report on electrically powered vehicles that did not require track, i.e. trolleybuses. Nothing came of this initiative and the subject of trolleybuses did not surface again until later.

In 1909, the Corporation decided to apply for powers to provide petrol bus or trolleybus services to areas around the town, with the Bill being published in November 1910. Of the feeder routes applied for, three were granted as indicated below:

From the Kimberworth tram terminus to Hesley Lane (Thorpe Hesley)
From the extended tramway in Broom Road to Westfield House, Maltby
From the Canklow tram terminus to Mill Lane, Treeton

The earliest trolleybuses had been developed on the continent, and the first British demonstration was in September 1909 at the Municipal Tramways Association Annual Conference. It was held at the Hendon depot of the Metropolitan Electric Tramway Company using a Railless Electric Traction (RET) vehicle. A contingent from Rotherham attended and was suitably impressed, presumably leading to the Corporation seeking the trolleybus powers indicated above.

The first British trolleybus systems opened on the same day in Bradford and Leeds on 20th June 1911, but Rotherham could not start their system until after 1st January 1912. This was presumably to allow the Board of Trade time to assess the success, or otherwise, of these two fledgling systems.

The first Rotherham route had been intended to run from the extended Broom Road tramway to the mining village of Maltby, a distance of 4.75 miles (7.6 km), the majority being outside the borough boundary. Rotherham became the fourth British trolleybus system to open, and was the first to operate outside borough boundaries.

The foundations of the Broom Road tramway extension had not settled sufficiently to install track, so permission was sought to temporarily move the start of the trollcybus route 0.63 miles (1.0 km) towards Rotherham. Permission was granted, and the route opened for service on 3rd October 1912 using three single deck RET vehicles.

Three further RET vehicles were ordered, but the 1914-1918 War took its toll, both with vehicle maintenance due to lack of spares, and staff shortages resulting from army recruitment.

Although there were discussions to extend the tramway to Maltby, trolleybus wiring was extended back into the Rotherham town centre to provide a 7 mile (11.3 km) through service to Maltby in January 1924. Later short working termini were provided at Stag Inn, Brecks Lane, Wickersley and Bramley. Initially the trolleybuses ran in parallel with the Broom Road trams, but the latter ceased in June 1929.

The Mexborough and Swinton tramway system operated in an area to the north of Rotherham, which included a joint service into the town via Parkgate. The company was also an early user of trolleybuses with two separate routes being opened in 1915. Full conversion of the system to trolleybuses began in 1928, and on 10th March 1929 (opening ceremony 2 days later), the final stage was implemented providing joint trolleybus operation into Rotherham town centre. Rotherham provided four Guy single deckers that travelled out to Rawmarsh and through Mexborough to Conisbrough Low. A later short extension along Adwick Road provided a turning facility in Mexborough.

During the 1920s, trolleybuses were ordered from Straker-Clough, some of which replaced the original RET vehicles.

The next conversion was the route between Thrybergh and Kimberworth (Colin Campbell pub), opening on 17th May 1931, and quickly followed by a branch to the Silverwood Colliery, utilising a batch of twenty-two RSJ single deck vehicles. On the Thrybergh section, a terminal loop was provided in 1933 for short workings to the Pumping Station from both directions.

Two tram routes remained, namely to Canklow and Templeborough/Tinsley, the latter being on the joint tram route to Sheffield. The Canklow route was converted to motorbus, whilst Sheffield would not agree to operate trolleybuses on the joint service, resulting in the tramway continuing between the two towns, and Rotherham ordering the eleven single ended tramcars.

A new section of wiring was opened on 28th March 1935, branching off the Maltby route along Broom Lane and then Bawtry Road, back to the main road at Brecks Lane. The final pre 1939-1945 War extension was to Greasbrough commencing in July 1936. Trams had operated neither of these extensions.

During the 1930s, Rotherham continued to take delivery of single deck central entrance trolleybuses from Guy plus AEC, and placed an order with Sunbeam in 1939, which was delivered in 1940. A further delivery of Sunbeams arrived in 1942.

The first trolleybus closure came on 7th February 1939, when the loop from the Maltby route to

Brecks Lane via Broom Lane was cut back to Worry Goose Lane.

With the increase in wartime production from the factories in the Templeborough area, trolleybus wiring was erected to the borough boundary running along side the tram service to Sheffield. This was in place by January 1940, and allowed cross-town workman services to Templeborough from various areas of the town, although the wiring was removed by November 1949.

The only post 1939-1945 War extension was to Toll Bar on the Kimberworth service, which opened in May 1948; it was short lived, being cut back to the short working terminus at Ewers Road in September 1953.

There was a need to replace the majority of the pre war fleet, and forty four Daimler single deck central entrance vehicles were ordered, and delivered in 1949 and 1950.

During 1951 trolleybuses ceased to operate on both the Greasbrough and Worry Goose Lane services. In 1954 the Maltby service was cut back to Wickersley, with the short working to Brecks Lane being retained.

The use of a low seating single deck fleet was proving uneconomic, and a new manager recommended the use of double deck vehicles. Twenty of the single deck Daimlers were selected and re-bodied into double deck format, entering service in 1956/57; this gave the system a temporary new lease of life. Eight of the single deck vehicles were retained to operate over the Mexborough and Swinton system, which was plagued with low bridges. A number of others were sold to Spanish operators. In March 1961, the Mexborough and Swinton trolleybus system closed, removing the need for Rotherham to operate single deck vehicles.

Finally, on 2nd October 1965, the Kimberworth-Thrybergh/Silverwood Colliery services were closed, bringing to an end 62 years of electrically power public transport in the town and surrounding area, which included 53 years of trolleybus operation.

Note on Fleet Numbering

The renumbering of vehicles during their lifetime stemmed mainly from the Corporation's desire to number the whole fleet, including trams, trolleybuses and buses, in a single series with no gaps. Another reason resulted from the renumbering of remaining vehicles when the balance of the batch had been withdrawn. In most instances, early/later fleet numbers have been included in the photograph captions, but in the minority of cases the renumbering was so substantial it is beyond the scope of this publication.

Service Numbers	Later 7/49	Earlier 10/29
Maltby	1	23
Brecks Lane	2 then 4	30
Wickersley	3	28
Bramley	-	22
Stag Inn (Broom)	4	21
Worry Goose Lane	4	32
Kimberworth - Toll Bar	5	11
Pumping Station	5	11
Kimberworth - Colin Campbell	-	12/10/11
Kimberworth - Ewers Road	6	12
Thrybergh	6	11 then 12
Greasbrough	7	26
Munsbrough Lane	-	33
Rawmarsh - Kilnhurst Road	8	24
Mexborough - Adwick Road	8 then 9	25
Silverwood	39 then 49	9
Templeborough	-	70?
Conisbrough Low	9	25

Liveries	Original	Chocolate & Yellow
	Later	Prussian Blue & Ivory
	Final	Azure Blue & Cream

Abbreviations

AEC	Associated Equipment Company (bus & trolleybus chassis)
BTH	British Thomson-Houston (trolleybus electrical equipment)
ECC	Electric Construction Company (trolleybus electric motors)
EEC	English Electric Company (trolleybus electrical equipment & bodywork)
GEC	General Electric Company (trolleybus electrical equipment)
NTA	National Trolleybus Association
OTA	Online Transport Archive
RET	Railless Electric Traction (early trolleybus)
RSJ	Ransomes Sims and Jefferies (trolleybus, electrical equipment & bodywork)

ROTHERHAM
CORPORATION TRANSPORT
Trolleybus Routes
Map 1

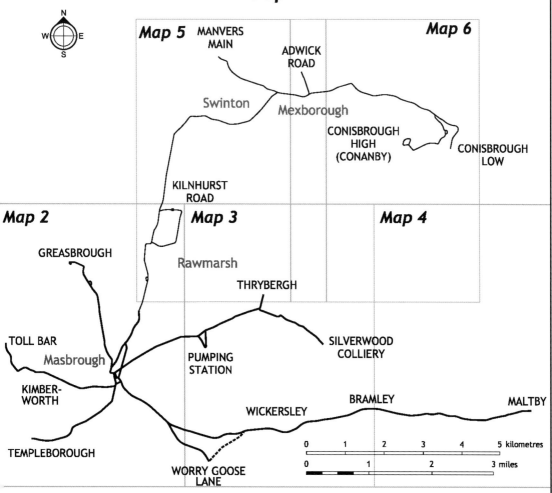

Map 5 MANVERS MAIN
ADWICK ROAD
Swinton
Mexborough
Map 6
CONISBROUGH HIGH (CONANBY)
CONISBROUGH LOW
KILNHURST ROAD

Map 2
GREASBROUGH
Map 3
Rawmarsh
THRYBERGH
Map 4

TOLL BAR
Masbrough
PUMPING STATION
SILVERWOOD COLLIERY
KIMBER-WORTH
BRAMLEY
MALTBY
WICKERSLEY
TEMPLEBOROUGH
WORRY GOOSE LANE

| 0 | 1 | 2 | 3 | 4 | 5 kilometres |
| 0 | | 1 | | 2 | 3 miles |

Legend - Map 1

——————— Rotherham Corporation trolleybus wiring

------------- Rotherham Corporation trolleybus route closed February 1939

——————— Mexborough & Swinton Traction Company trolleybus wiring

Legend - Maps 2 to 6

 Rotherham Corporation trolleybus wiring and Mexborough & Swinton Traction Company trolleybus wiring used by Rotherham Corporation, as in 1944

Mexborough & Swinton Traction Company trolleybus wiring used only by M & S services

⑫ (12) original service number   6 | 6 | later service number   A /A\ Mexborough & Swinton service letter

--------- route of former tramway and original trolleybus route

+-+-+-+ route of former Dearne District Light Railway, 1924 - 1933

——————— other roads

——————— main line railway and station

Based on J.C.Gillham's Map No.264, d/d 07/1961
and E.M.H.Humphreys' N.T.A. Record map (no date).
© C.Barker and R.A.Smith, 05/2013. No.1410, v1.2.

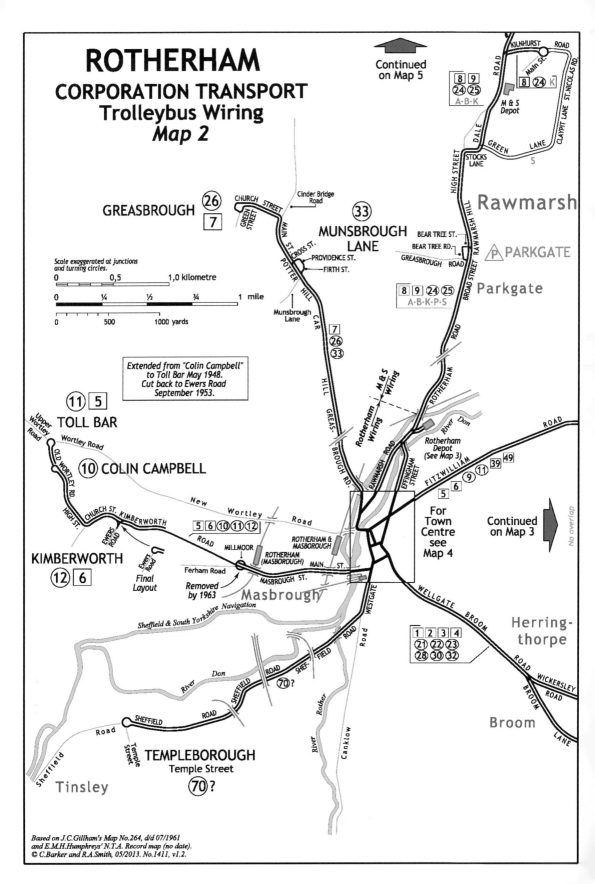

ROTHERHAM
CORPORATION TRANSPORT
Trolleybus Wiring
Map 2

Continued on Map 5

⑧ ⑨
㉔ ㉕
A·B·K

⑧ ㉔ K

KILNHURST ROAD
Main St.

M & S Depot

STOCKS LANE

GREEN LANE S

HIGH STREET

DALE ROAD

CLAYPIT LANE · ST.NICOLAS RD.

Rawmarsh

GREASBROUGH ⑳ ⑦
CHURCH STREET
GREEN STREET
Cinder Bridge Road

㉝
MUNSBROUGH LANE
PROVIDENCE ST.
FIRTH ST.
CROSS ST.

MAIN ST.

POTTER HILL

BEAR TREE ST.
BEAR TREE RD.
GREASBROUGH ROAD

Ⓟ **PARKGATE**

RAWMARSH HILL

BROAD STREET

⑧ ⑨ ㉔ ㉕
A·B·K·P·S

Parkgate

Scale exaggerated at junctions and turning circles.

0   0,5   1,0 kilometre

0   ¼   ½   ¾   1 mile

0   500   1000 yards

GREAS-BROUGH CAR HILL

Munsbrough Lane

⑦
⑳
㉝

Box: *Extended from "Colin Campbell" to Toll Bar May 1948. Cut back to Ewers Road September 1953.*

⑪ ⑤
TOLL BAR
Upper Wortley Road
Wortley Road
OLD WORTLEY RD.

⑩ **COLIN CAMPBELL**

HIGH ST.
CHURCH ST. KIMBERWORTH
New   Wortley   Road

⑤ ⑥ ⑩ ⑪ ⑫
ROAD
MILLMOOR
ROTHERHAM & MASBOROUGH

KIMBERWORTH
⑫ ⑥
EWERS ROAD
Ewers Road
Final Layout
Ferham Road
Removed by 1963
ROTHERHAM (MASBOROUGH)
MASBROUGH ST.
MAIN ST.
Masbrough

M & S Wiring
Rotherham Wiring

RAWMARSH ROAD
EFFINGHAM STREET
ROTHERHAM ROAD

River Don

Rotherham Depot (See Map 3)

FITZWILLIAM
⑨ ⑪ ㊴ ㊾
⑤ ⑥

For Town Centre see Map 4

Continued on Map 3

No overlap

ROAD

Sheffield & South Yorkshire Navigation

River Don

BROUGH RD.

FIELD ROAD
SHEFFIELD ROAD
WESTGATE

Road

River Rother
Canklow

WELLGATE
BROOM ROAD

① ② ③ ④
㉑ ㉒ ㉓
㉘ ㉚ ㉜

WICKERSLEY ROAD
BROOM LANE

Herring-thorpe

Broom

SHEFFIELD   ROAD
⑦⓪?

Temple Street
Sheffield Road

TEMPLEBOROUGH
Temple Street
⑦⓪?

Tinsley

Based on J.C.Gillham's Map No.264, d/d 07/1961 and E.M.H.Humphreys' N.T.A. Record map (no date). © C.Barker and R.A.Smith, 05/2013. No.1411, v1.2.

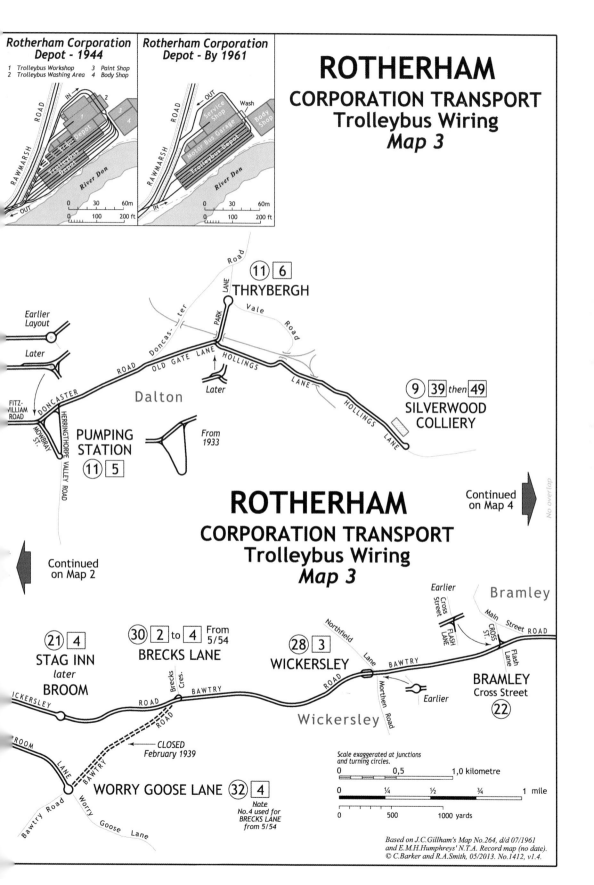

Rotherham Corporation Depot - 1944

1 Trolleybus Workshop
2 Trolleybus Washing Area
3 Paint Shop
4 Body Shop

RAWMARSH ROAD
IN
OUT
River Don

0 30 60m
0 100 200 ft

Rotherham Corporation Depot - By 1961

RAWMARSH ROAD
OUT
IN
Service Shop
Motor Bus Garage
Trolleybus Depot
Wash
Body Shop
River Don

0 30 60m
0 100 200 ft

ROTHERHAM
CORPORATION TRANSPORT
Trolleybus Wiring
Map 3

Road
Lane

⑪ 6
THRYBERGH

PARK LANE
Vale Road

Doncas-ter

OLD GATE LANE
HOLLINGS

ROAD
Later
HOLLINGS LANE

Dalton

⑨ 39 *then* 49
SILVERWOOD COLLIERY

FITZ-WILLIAM ROAD
DONCASTER
MOWBRAY ST.
HERRINGTHORPE VALLEY ROAD

Earlier Layout

Later

PUMPING STATION
⑪ 5

From 1933

ROTHERHAM
CORPORATION TRANSPORT
Trolleybus Wiring
Map 3

Continued on Map 4

No overlap

Continued on Map 2

Bramley

Earlier
Cross Street
FLASH LANE
Main Street ROAD
CROSS ST.
Flash Lane

㉑ 4
STAG INN
later
BROOM

㉚ 2 to 4 From 5/54
BRECKS LANE

Northfield Lane

㉘ 3
WICKERSLEY

BAWTRY

ROAD
Morthen Road

Earlier

BRAMLEY
Cross Street
㉒

ICKERSLEY
ROAD
Brecks Cres.
BAWTRY ROAD
ROAD

Wickersley

ROOM
LANE
BAWTRY

CLOSED February 1939

Bawtry Road
Worry Goose Lane

WORRY GOOSE LANE ㉜ 4

Note
No.4 used for
BRECKS LANE
from 5/54

Scale exaggerated at junctions and turning circles.

0   0,5   1,0 kilometre

0   ¼   ½   ¾   1 mile

0   500   1000 yards

Based on J.C.Gillham's Map No.264, d/d 07/1961
and E.M.H.Humphreys' N.T.A. Record map (no date).
© C.Barker and R.A.Smith, 05/2013. No.1412, v1.4.

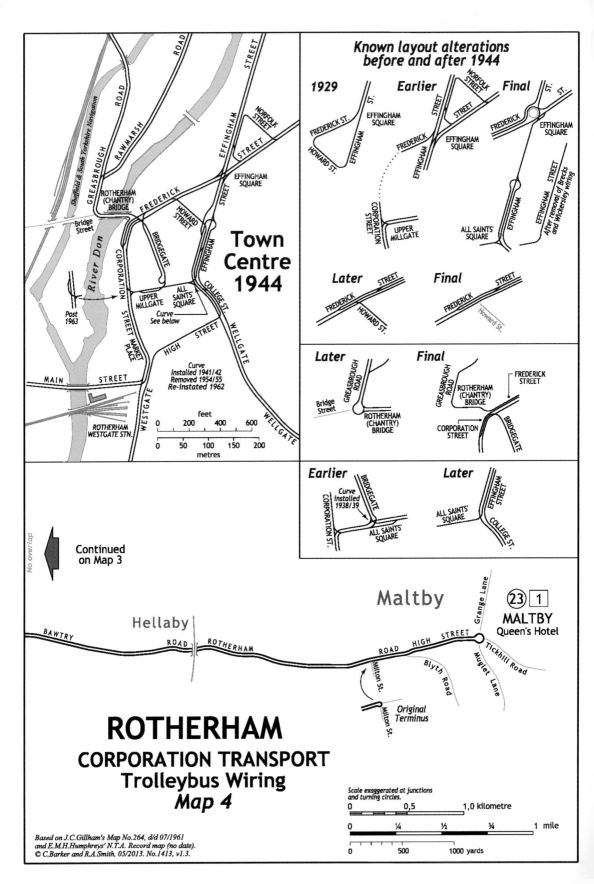

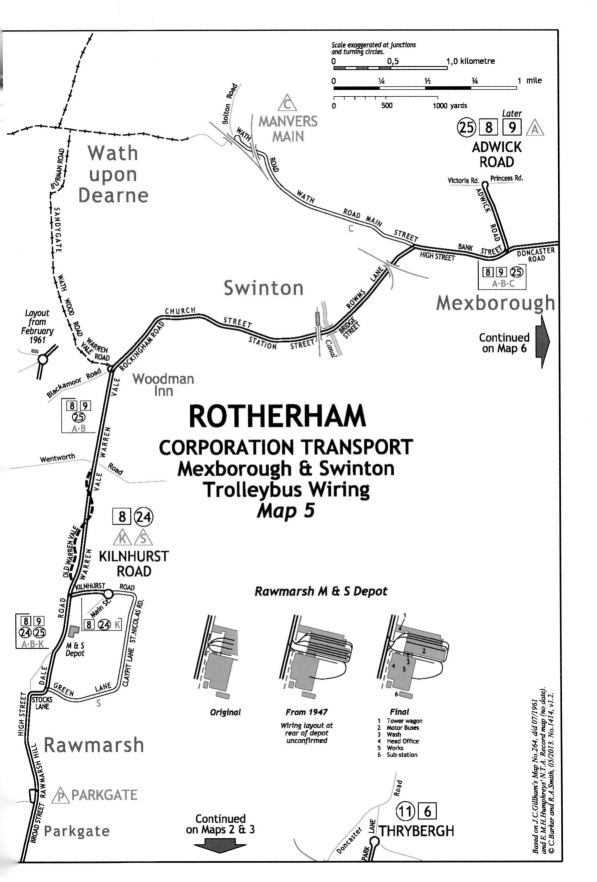

Scale exaggerated at junctions and turning circles.

0   0,5   1,0 kilometre

0   ¼   ½   ¾   1 mile

0   500   1000 yards

Bolton Road

MANVERS MAIN

△C

WATH ROAD

Later
㉕ 8 9 △A

ADWICK ROAD

Victoria Rd.   Princess Rd.

ADWICK ROAD

BURMAN ROAD

Wath upon Dearne

SANDYGATE

WATH WOOD ROAD

WATH ROAD MAIN STREET

C

HIGH STREET   BANK STREET   DONCASTER ROAD

Swinton

Mexborough

8 9 ㉕
A·B·C

Continued on Map 6 ➡

CHURCH STREET

STATION STREET   Canal

BRIDGE STREET   ROWMS LANE

Layout from February 1961

WARREN VALE ROAD

ROCKINGHAM ROAD

Blackamoor Road

Woodman Inn

8 9
㉕
A·B

VALE   WARREN   Road

Wentworth

ROTHERHAM
CORPORATION TRANSPORT
Mexborough & Swinton
Trolleybus Wiring
Map 5

8 ㉔
△K △S

KILNHURST ROAD

OLD WARREN VALE

WARREN   ROAD

KILNHURST ROAD   Main St.   ST.NICOLAS RD.

8 ㉔ K

CLAYPIT LANE

8 9
㉔㉕
A·B·K

M & S Depot

DALE   GREEN   LANE

S

STOCKS LANE

HIGH STREET   RAWMARSH HILL

Rawmarsh

Rawmarsh M & S Depot

1
2
3
4 5
6

Original

From 1947

Wiring layout at rear of depot unconfirmed

Final

1 Tower wagon
2 Motor Buses
3 Wash
4 Head Office
5 Works
6 Sub-station

BROAD STREET

△P **PARKGATE**

Parkgate

Continued on Maps 2 & 3 ⬇

Doncaster Road   PARK LANE

⑪ 6
THRYBERGH

Based on J.C.Gillham's Map No.264, d'd 07/1961 and E.M.H.Humphreys' N.T.A. Record map (no date). © C.Barker and R.A.Smith, 05/2013. No.1414, v1.2.

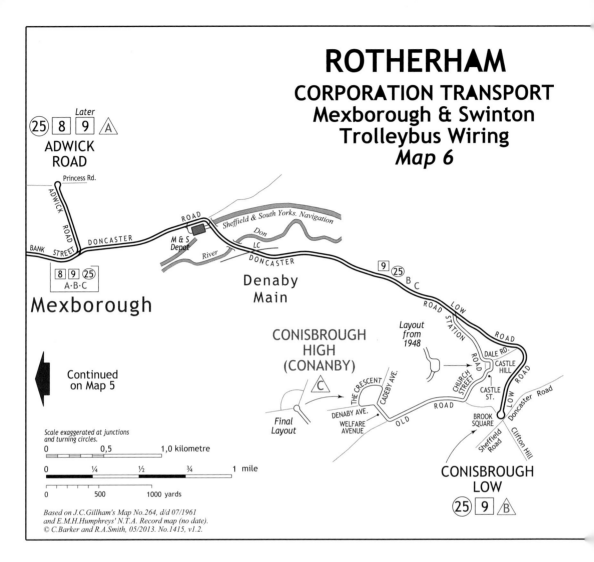

ROTHERHAM
CORPORATION TRANSPORT
Mexborough & Swinton
Trolleybus Wiring
Map 6

(25) 8 9 Ⓐ *Later*
ADWICK ROAD

Princess Rd.

ADWICK ROAD

ROAD

DONCASTER

BANK STREET

M & S Depot

Sheffield & South Yorks. Navigation

Don

LC

River

DONCASTER

8 9 (25)
A·B·C

Mexborough

Denaby Main

CONISBROUGH HIGH (CONANBY)
Ⓒ

Continued on Map 5

Scale exaggerated at junctions and turning circles.

0   0,5   1,0 kilometre

0   ¼   ½   ¾   1 mile

0   500   1000 yards

9 (25)
B C

ROAD STATION

LOW ROAD

Layout from 1948

DALE RD.

CASTLE HILL

ROAD

CHURCH STREET

CASTLE ST.

LOW ROAD

Doncaster Road

THE CRESCENT

CADEBY AVE.

DENABY AVE.

WELFARE AVENUE

ROAD

OLD

BROOK SQUARE

Final Layout

Sheffield Road

Clifton Hill

CONISBROUGH LOW
(25) 9 Ⓑ

*Based on J.C.Gillham's Map No.264, d/d 07/1961
and E.M.H.Humphreys' N.T.A. Record map (no date).
© C.Barker and R.A.Smith, 05/2013. No.1415, v1.2.*

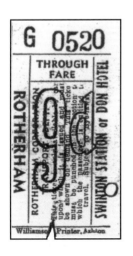

G 0520
THROUGH FARE
ROTHERHAM ... SWINTON STATION OR DON HOTEL
90
Williamson Printer, Ashton

Ap 0983
THROUGH FARE
HOLLY BUSH ... Rotherham Terminus to
4 1/2
Williamson, Printer, Ashton

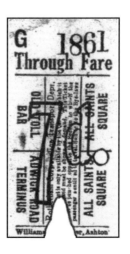

G 1861
Through Fare
OLD TOLL BAR ... ALL SAINTS SQUARE
ADWICK ROAD TERMINUS
7 1/2
Williamson, Printer, Ashton

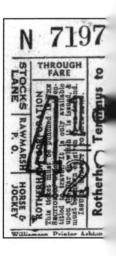

N 7197
THROUGH FARE
STOCKS LANE ... Rotherham Terminus to
RAWMARSH P.O. ... HORSE & JOCKEY
4 1/2
Williamson Printer Ashton

IN THE BEGINNING

1.	Rotherham's first trolleybus route was to the mining village of Maltby, providing a connecting service from the Broom Road tram terminus. At the time it was the longest trolleybus route in the country at 4.75 miles (7.6 km) long, with the majority outside the town boundary. Initially, there was a 0.63 mile (1.0 km) temporary increase at the town end because the extension to the Broom Road tram service could not be completed, as the new road surface had not settled sufficiently to allow for the laying of track. This view depicts the well supported opening ceremony on 3rd October 1912, with the first three Railless trolleybuses at the temporary Broom Road terminus, and two trams in the background. (S Lockwood collection)

2.	Another view of the opening ceremony with the three vehicles in view. At the time of introduction, vehicle registration numbers were not required, and only implemented in 1921. Fleet numbers 38-40 were initially allocated, but subsequently changed to T1-T3. Three similar vehicles were introduced in 1913, and it was not until 1921 that any further trolleybuses entered service. Both 38 and 39 were demonstrated in Sheffield, but the city continued to rely on trams for its electrically powered public transport. See pictures 37 & 99. (NTA)

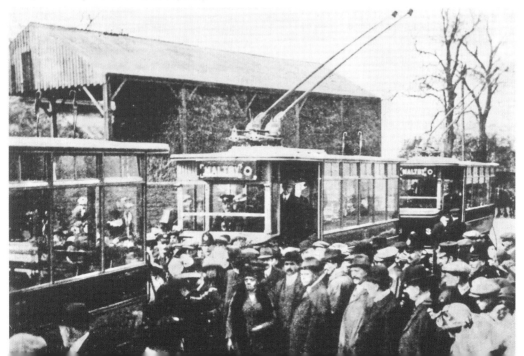

EFFINGHAM SQUARE

3.   Daimler 85 (later double deck 26), in as delivered livery, crosses Effingham Square along Frederick Street in 1950, which is intersected by Effingham Street. It is on a return trip from Pumping Station, and destined for Toll Bar, the short lived May 1948 extension of the Kimberworh service from the Colin Campbell public house; it was cut back to Ewers Road in September 1953. Wiring to the left along Effingham Street provided depot access/egress, and outward journeys to the northern territory of Mexborough and Swinton. Note the granite setts and tram track still in situ, with a Ford 5cwt van in the background. (C Carter)

→   4. Daimler 91 (later double deck 34), also in as delivered livery, waits at the traffic lights on the south side of the square before continuing along Frederick Street on the way to Kimberworth. The long established Jays furniture store provides the backdrop, advertising tax free exhibition furniture with payment by cash, or hire purchase. The granite setts and Austin Big Seven complete the picture. (D F Parker)

→   5. Victorian chimney pots reflect in the nearside windscreen of Daimler 90 as it passes through Effingham Square destined for Kimberworth. Behind is Sunbeam 62 (originally 73 and later 72), and on the left is AEC 48 (originally 67 and later 67) waiting on stand for an outward trip to Silverwood. To the rear of 62 is a right hand turn into the Silverwood terminal loop along Norfolk Street, Effingham Street and then to the stand indicated. 90 is in as delivered livery, with trafficators adjacent to the offside headlight, and was sold for further service in Cadiz, Spain. (C Carter)

6.　　The power station cooling towers dominate this view of Daimler 87, which also eventually saw service in Cadiz, waiting on the northern side of the square for a departure on Service 49 to Silverwood in July 1954. In later years, returning vehicles from Silverwood travelled along Effingham Street into All Saints Square, and then onto stand in Corporation Street. In 1931, when the Silverwood service began, it started from All Saints Square, but was quickly moved to Effingham Square. A Mexborough and Swinton Sunbeam moves north along Effingham Street on an outward trip to its home territory. Also in the picture is Rotherham motorbus Bristol LG5 149 (originally 106), which was rebodied to that illustrated by East Lancashire Coachbuilders (Bridlington) in 1952.
(J Copland/A D Packer copyright))

➜　　7. At the same location AEC 48 (originally 67, and later 67) waits for an outward trip to Silverwood, whilst displaying an earlier service number 39. Woodley furniture stores predominate, and there is a Radio Times advertisement on the wall above the trolleybus roof mounted resistors. The overhead wiring curving out of the northern section of Effingham Street was the end of the terminal loop described earlier, and also provided egress from the depot to this stand.
(C Carter)

➜　　8. The square was transformed by a traffic management scheme in 1962, which created an island following some building demolition. Daimler 44 (originally single deck 18) is slightly forward of the position seen in Picture 4, with Jays store on the right, next to Easiephit. The north eastern section of Frederick Street stretches back towards Fitzwilliam Road. The overhead wiring on the right, with the curved segment twin line hanger, led to the southern section of Effingham Street. Note the Heinkel bubble car bringing up the rear. (Travel Lens Photographic)

9.   In this view, the traffic island and approaches are "work in progress", as Daimler 42 (originally single deck 14) moves to the south western section of Frederick Street on the way to Kimberworth. The Melias store is on the corner of the southern section of Effingham Street, and an Armstrong Siddley saloon can be seen in the background. (V Nutton/Travel Lens Photographic)

EFFINGHAM STREET

The group of services that left the town centre via Wellgate and Broom Road, in the Maltby direction, terminated in Effingham Street. Trolleybuses to the Pumping Station also passed along this thoroughfare to reach All Saints Square from Effingham Square.

10.   Daimler 88, eventually to operate in Cadiz, turns round in Effingham Street at the junction with Howard Street at lunchtime in April 1954, before making a return trip to Maltby. A similar inward bound vehicle is about to leave the continuation of Effingham Street from Effingham Square, eventually destined for Pumping Station. The Symbol Biscuits van waits to execute a right turn, with the driver about to make a hand signal. Top right, one of the power station cooling towers can just be seen.
(J Copland/A D Packer copyright)

11.   Guy 43 (earlier 203, 13, 52 and subsequently 65) is seen on the stand for Maltby circa 1948/49, having completed the turning manoeuvre seen in the previous picture. The stand display indicates Service 23 for Maltby, and Service 22 for Bramley, the latter a short working between Wickersley and Maltby. These service numbers are from an earlier series. Note the front roof mounted resistors, and the overhead wiring leading out of Howard Street on the left. The building on the corner of Howard Street is the Mechanics Institute and Assembly Rooms opened in October 1853, and now houses a number of retail outlets at street level. See Picture 108 where resistors were originally under the rear seating. (W J Haynes)

➔ 12. Daimler 40 (originally single deck 8) loads ready for a lunchtime departure to Wickersley, with the front offside wing needing attention. The trolleybuses never carried external advertisements, although agreed to by the Transport Committee in 1962, thereby foregoing a source of revenue that the system could have benefited from in later years. (PM Photos)

➔   13. Also destined for Wickersley is Sunbeam 73 (originally 88 and subsequently 74), with the erstwhile Woolworth's store behind. This vehicle was removed from a local rifle club, where it had resided after withdrawal, and is undergoing long term restoration by members of the Rotherham Trolleybus Group. Also see Picture 117. (S Lockwood collection)

14.   On an extremely wet day, Daimler 39 (originally single deck 82) pauses on the last stage of the turning manoeuvre, before reaching the stand for the Brecks Lane short working. The overhead wiring from the upper part of Effingham Street, that joins the nearside wires above 39, allowed vehicles to enter service from the depot, having travelled through Effingham Square. The printing works of Henry Garnett provides the backdrop, whilst the newspaper seller on the right makes a sale, probably the "Rotherham Advertiser". (D F Parker)

→   15. With the Old College Inn on the right, Daimler 44 (originally single deck 18) rounds the bend into College Street on the short working to Brecks Lane. An early Land Rover, an Austin Devon A40 saloon and a Rotherham Bristol motorbus complete the picture. This vehicle operated on an enthusiasts' special the day after the system closed on 2nd October 1965. It was saved after withdrawal, and is now in store awaiting restoration. (R Brook/P Watson copyright)

→   16. Guy 34 (originally 64) has completed the turn, and waits to move to the Worry Goose Lane stand post May 1949. This service left the main route to Maltby and travelled along Broom Lane to the junction with Bawtry Road. When introduced in March 1935, the service continued along Bawtry Road to rejoin the main route at Brecks Lane. However, the service was cut back to terminate at Worry Goose Lane in February 1939. (C Carter)

ALL SAINTS SQUARE/UPPER MILLGATE

17.	Ransomes 34 (subsequent renumbering uncertain) is seen in this pre war view entering All Saints Square, with the conductor ensuring he gets in the picture. At this stage, the Kimberworth service passed through the square, and the earlier service number 12 is displayed. Overhead wiring out of the square into Effingham Street can be seen top left, and in the background another trolleybus with a Sheffield tram on the joint service. (Author's collection)

➡	18. An early 1930s view of the square with Guy 43 on the left, one of the four purchased in 1928/29 for the joint services with Mexborough and Swinton. To the right is Ransomes 25 (later 33 and then 16) destined for Kimberworth. An indication of the fashions of the time are the headdress and cane basket of the lady on the left. The joint services originally entered the town centre via Effingham Street, and then along Howard Street to reach the stands in Frederick Street. They were subsequently moved to All Saints Square, as indicated above, and left via Bridgegate/Frederick Street. To ease congestion in the square, a further alteration resulted in vehicles entering and leaving by Bridgegate, having arrived by Rawmarsh Road, and using a turning circle adjacent to the square. Finally, the stands were returned to Frederick Street. (NTA)

➡	19. Daimler 30 (originally single deck 79) waits on stand, with the driver and conductor enjoying a quick chat through the bulkhead opening window, before returning to Pumping Station. To the rear, is a Daimler single deck vehicle, with the Old College Inn beyond. Effingham Street is to the left of the hostelry, and College Street to the right. (S J Butler collection)

20.   A wonderful animated wartime scene of the square, with four trolleybuses and two motorbuses in view. In the foreground, is Sunbeam 83 (later 68) with an earlier Maltby service number, suggesting an incorrect display from this location. On the left, Guy 22 (later 58 and then 71) makes the turn out of Bridgegate into Upper Millgate on return from Greasbrough. To the rear of 83 is Bristol motorbus 106 (later 149); this vehicle was rebodied in 1952, and eventually became a Corporation Welfare Department ambulance in 1960. This maybe a posed photograph. (D J Richardson collection)

↗ 21.   Two Ransomes trolleybuses are depicted in this 1930s view of the square. On the right is 36 destined for Kimberworth, whilst 29 on the left is about to leave Upper Millgate for Thrybergh, passing through the square and into Effingham Street. Circa 1938/39, the stand was moved round the corner into Bridgegate, with vehicles leaving via Frederick Street/Effingham Square. Finally, the Kimberworth/Thrybergh service travelled the length of Corporation Street, thus avoiding All Saints Square. One of the Guy six wheel vehicles, purchased for the Mexborough/Conisbrough services, is in the background. (Commercial postcard/Author's collection)

➔   22.   Daimler 33 (originally single deck 93) leaves the square, travelling towards Corporation Street, and enters Upper Millgate outward bound for Pumping Station. There is now only single overhead wiring in this thoroughfare, as a Rotherham motorbus waits outside the White Hart Hotel, which is now a solicitor's office, although the original signage can still be seen over the right hand roof arch.   The erstwhile Greasbrough service terminated on the right. (J Copland/A D Packer copyright)

Newspaper cutting February 1962

CORPORATION STREET

23.   After a heavy shower, Daimler 31 (originally single deck 15) turns out of Upper Millgate into the northern section of Corporation Street, outward bound for Pumping Station. On the right is motorbus Bristol 199 destined for Canklow, a tram service not converted to trolleybus operation. All Saints Square can be seen in the distance between the two vehicles. The overhead wiring top right led into the southern part of Corporation Street, whilst on the left is the Turf Tavern public house. (Author's collection)

➜   24. Having exited Upper Millgate on the left, Daimler 39 (originally single deck 82), also destined for Pumping Station, waits under the overhead loop adjacent to an inconveniently parked Ford Anglia van. A sister vehicle for Thrybergh is to the rear in this October 1965 view. When the layover for Pumping Station was in All Saints Square, there was just a trailing junction in the overhead wiring at this point, but it would appear that crew breaks were now being taken at this location. The overhead wiring loop allowed vehicles from Kimberworth bound for Thrybergh to overtake any trolleybus on the Pumping Station stand. The property on the facing corner has been demolished, providing a stunning view of Rotherham Minster, previously known as All Saints Church. (J Copland/A D Packer copyright)

➜   25. An immaculate Daimler 37 (originally single deck 17) waits at the Thrybergh stand opposite Upper Millgate; this is the location of the rear vehicle in the previous picture. This vehicle has been restored, and is operational at the Trolleybus Museum, Sandtoft, North Lincolnshire. (J Fozard)

26.   A dirty Daimler 12 (later double deck 32) in as delivered livery, waits at the Kimberworth stand in the southern section of Corporation Street, just round the corner from Upper Millgate. The conscientious driver has placed a chock under the front wheel, given that the road to the rear has an adverse incline. The products sold in the Rhodes shop would be more likely to be found in one of the DIY stores today. (D F Parker)

➔   27. Daimler 30 (originally single deck 79) on its way to Thrybergh, leaves Corporation Street and is about to enter Frederick Street, which was the departure point for Mexborough/Conisbrough services in the early and later years. The right hand overhead wiring was the end of the terminal loop from Rawmarsh Road for these services; the Bridge Inn on the opposite side of Chantry Bridge is in the right background. The overhead wiring curving to the left led into Bridgegate. (R F Mack)

➔   28. A little further along Frederick Street, Daimler 1 (originally 24) has the destination blind set for a return trip to Mexborough, Adwick Road. The service number 9 was used in later years for this destination and Conisbrough Low, whilst originally it was service 8. This vehicle was one of those sold for further service in Lasarte/San Sebastian, Spain in 1960. Note the Ford Anglia to the rear. (Author's collection)

29.   Vehicles on the joint services to the north of the town are depicted in this view taken circa 1949. In the foreground is Guy 28 (earlier 16 and later 60), followed by a Mexborough and Swinton Sunbeam, against the background of Water Works buildings that made way for shops, and the Rotherham Interchange. (C Carter)

OUTWARDS TOWARDS MALTBY

The service to Maltby opened on 3rd October 1912, with subsequent turning facilities being provided at Stag Inn, Brecks Lane, Wickersley and Bramley. The Maltby section was cut back to Wickersley on 2nd May 1954, and the remaining line closed on 13th January 1963.

Brecks Lane

↖ 30. Daimler 34 (originally single deck 91), seen here returning to the town centre from Wickersley, has entered Wickersley Road from Bawtry Road in the background. The road entering the traffic island from the right is East Bawtry Road, which is where the pre war service from Worry Goose Lane joined the main route to Maltby. The Brecks Lane short working terminus is in the far distance.
(P Mitchell)

31.　　　Daimler 9 (later 5) passes the Rotherham boundary on route to Maltby in April 1954, with the Brecks Hotel, now known as "The Brecks", in the background. The Brecks Lane terminus was just to the right of the picture. (J Copland/A D Packer copyright)

32.　　　The Brecks Hotel can be seen again on the immediate right, with Daimler 41 (originally single deck 11) standing in the untidy short working turning circle adjacent to Brecks Crescent in March 1962. The road is deserted other than the car leaving the end of the dual carriageway.
(J Copland/A D Packer copyright)

33.   On the same day, 41 is about to complete the Brecks Lane turning manoeuvre to begin the return trip back to the town centre. On the left is the Bawtry Road Service Station. Note that a passenger shelter has been erected in the eight years since the next picture, and that the road towards Maltby is devoid of traffic. (J Copland/A D Packer copyright)

34.   Daimler 88, which saw later service in Cadiz, passes the Brecks Lane turning circle in April 1954 on a return trip from Wickersley. Note the absence of a passenger shelter, and again the lack of traffic.   (J Copland/A D Packer copyright)

Wickersley

35. Having just left Wickersley to return to town, Daimler 29 (originally single deck 75), now reaches the district of Listerdale, with Sledgate Lane to the right of the motorcyclist. (P Mitchell)

36. Here we see the Wickersley turning circle adjacent to Morthern Road in April 1954, with the overhead wiring continuing along Bawtry Road towards Bramley and Maltby. The circle crossed both sets of through wiring, allowing vehicles turning here to lay over, whilst not impeding overtaking trolleybuses to/from the Maltby direction. Daimler 9 (later 5) waits, having made the turn, but showing an incorrect service number, possibly changed for the next outward journey. (J Copland/A D Packer copyright)

37.   This rear view of Railless 39 in Wickersley, which was one of the original vehicles, illustrates the open platform and fabricated steps. The solid tyres had an adverse effect on the road surface of the period. The skate below the rear platform was towed in the tram track to provide a negative return, whilst using single tram overhead when travelling to and from the depot/Stag Inn. (Author's collection)

38.   Daimler 36 (originally single deck 92) makes the turn back to town, with the overhead wiring to Maltby removed. Splicing ears in the overhead wiring can just be seen where an outward crossover has been removed. Only the house to the rear of 36 is identifiable today, with the road now being dual carriageway leading to a large traffic island on the right. (V Nutton/Travel Lens Photographic)

Maltby

39.   The Maltby service opened on 3rd October 1912 and here we see Railless 39, one of the initial six trolleybuses, waiting at the original terminus. This was at Westfield House adjacent to Milton Street, which was some way from the village centre. A passenger shelter was provided behind 39 at a later date and a tower wagon can be seen on the extreme left. (Rotherham Archives and Local Studies Service)

40.   The service was extended into the centre of Maltby in December 1924, and here we see Daimler 92 (later double deck 36) making its way along High Street, a short distance from the new terminus at the Queens Hotel. The building on the left, with a semi-circular roof, was originally a billiards hall, and is currently a "One Stop" store. (C Carter)

41.   The Maltby terminus was at the junction of High Street, Tickhill Road, Muglet Lane and Grange Lane adjacent to the Queens Hotel. Daimler 87, subsequently sold to Spain, completes the turn back, with Grange Lane facing. Note the gas lamp and telegraph pole on the right. (Omnibus Society copyright)

42. With the Queens Hotel as a backdrop, and Muglet Lane on the right, Daimler 92 (later double deck 36) is seen in as delivered livery waiting on stand before making the return to Rotherham. The hotel has recently been refurbished by Wetherspoons. (H Luff/OTA)

Worry Goose Lane

This service began on 28th March 1935 through to Brecks Lane, but was cut back to Worry Goose Lane on 7th February 1939; the service ceased on 30th June 1951.

43.   We return to the Worry Goose Lane branch, (although out of implementation date sequence) with Daimler 88 in as delivered livery, leaving Broom Road to travel along Broom Lane to the terminus at the junction with Bawtry Road. This vehicle was fitted with Crompton Parkinson electrical equipment, but the photograph was commissioned by English Electric. The latter's Publicity Department made the mistake, presumably to the satisfaction of the Crompton Parkinson staff. When first opened, the service left Broom Lane and travelled along Bawtry Road to join the main route at Brecks Lane. (English Electric/ D Beilby collection)

44.   Daimler 88 is seen again at the Worry Goose Lane terminus, with the turning circle around the traffic island in the background, which is at the junction with Bawtry Road. Vehicles turned left here to reach Brecks Lane before the pre-war cut back to this location. (English Electric/ D Beilby collection)

JOINT SERVICES WITH MEXBOROUGH
AND SWINTON TRACTION

*The joint services commenced on 10th March 1929 (opening ceremony two days later)
and ceased on 26th March 1961.*

Rotherham (Outward)

45.   On leaving Frederick Street, the joint services with Mexborough and Swinton travelled north
along Effingham Street, and then turned left over Grafton Bridge, officially known as Don Bridge, which
is the location of this view of Daimler 6 (originally 10) outward bound for Mexborough. This was the
last leg of the terminal loop through the town centre, with the left hand overhead wiring providing egress
from the Rotherham depot in Rawmarsh Road, which is to the left of the photographer's position. In the
background is the Grafton Hotel and this, plus all the surrounding buildings, have disappeared to make
way for a major road scheme, including a new river bridge; the old bridge has been removed in the recent
past. (P.Mitchell)

46.　　Guy 29 (originally 17 and later 61) leaves Grafton Bridge, circa 1949, to turn into Rawmarsh Road and will then immediately pass the Rotherham depot on the way to Conisbrough Low. Note the vertical boom tension springs specified on all pre-war vehicles.　(R Marshall)

Parkgate

47.　　After leaving Rotherham, the next port of call was Parkgate at the bottom of Rawmarsh Hill, where a "round the houses" short working was provided. The loop turned left off Broad Street into Greasbrough Road, and then a right hand circuit via Bear Tree Road and Bear Tree Street before rejoining the main line. Daimler 3 (originally 6) is seen in Bear Tree Street, before reaching the main road on an enthusiasts' tour on 26th March 1961. Heinz products are still with us. (R F Mack/NTA collection)

48.   After passing through Rawmarsh centre, and the Mexborough and Swinton depot in Dale Road (see front cover), vehicles could turn right off the main route into Kilnhurst Road to terminate a little further along in the Ryecroft district. In this view, Daimler 3 is seen again, about to leave Kilnhurst Road and turn into Dale Road back towards Rotherham. The turning circle is in the distance, where Mexborough vehicles could approach from the opposite direction, and having turned at the same point, return along a loop including Green Lane, Nicolas Road and Clay Pit Lane to re-join the main route at the junction of Stocks Lane and Dale Road. This service from Rotherham was the sole preserve of the Mexborough company. (J C Gillham)

49.   After leaving the junction with Kilnhurst Road, vehicles for Mexborough and Conisbrough Low entered Warren Vale, the fairly rural section of this otherwise urban trolleybus system. The road continued to the Woodman Inn, the past terminus of the short lived Dearne District Light Railway cars, which had travelled from the Wath direction. In an almost deserted Warren Vale, looking towards Woodman, Daimlers 3 (originally 6) and 7 (originally 76) pass under 18ins (457mm) spaced overhead wiring. (V Nutton/Travel Lens Photographic)

50.	With the Swinton boundary in Rockingham Road on the right, Daimler 5 (originally 9) rounds the traffic island at Woodman Inn before entering Warren Vale, and then back to Rotherham in March 1961. The traffic island became operational in February 1961, and was therefore only used for a couple of months before closure of the system. The overhead wiring allowed turn back from either direction. (J Copland/A D Packer copyright)

51.	After arriving in Swinton, and dipping under the low railway bridge which carried the line from Rotherham north towards York, vehicles were immediately faced with a hump back bridge over the Dearne and Dove canal, part of the Sheffield and South Yorkshire Navigation. To the right of this location are the Swinton Locks leading to the Mexborough New Cut. Daimler 8 (originally 77) is about to crest the canal bridge and proceed along Bridge Street and Rowms Lane towards Mexborough. A full width bracket arm carries the overhead wiring over the bridge apex. (A B Cross)

Mexborough

52.   Daimler 6 (originally 10) passes under the two low railway bridges that necessitated the use of single deck trolleybuses on these services. The two bridges are at the end of Rowms Lane, looking along Swinton Road towards the centre of Mexborough; they carried ex Great Central Railway lines and had a headroom of 14ft 3ins (4.34 metres). (P Mitchell)

53.   Guy 57 (originally 21 and later 70) waits in Bank Street, Mexborough, before departing to Conisbrough Low post May 1949. Children's toys and baby equipment dominate the shop window display. (C Carter)

54.   In order to provide a turning facility in Mexborough, a branch was opened along Adwick Road on 28th June 1931, with a circle erected at the junction with Princess Road. This view depicts the start of the extension, with Adwick Road off to the left, and Doncaster Road to the right; Bank Street is to the rear of the photographer's position. Daimler 5 (originally 9) leaves Adwick Road in April 1960 to rejoin the main route back to Rotherham. A traffic island is now situated at this road junction. The Esso garage on the right is advertising Humber, Sunbeam and Hillman cars, makes that have long since disappeared. (J Copland/A D Packer copyright)

55.   At the Adwick Road turning circle, Daimlers 3 (originally 6), and 5 (originally 9), wait to return to Rotherham in the early afternoon, with the driver of the rear vehicle about to have a chat with his colleague. Both vehicles are displaying Service 9, the number also used for Conisbrough Low; earlier Adwick Road carried Service 8. There were plans to extend the overhead wiring further along Adwick Road to the Windhill Estate, but this was never implemented. Note the passenger shelter, the clock tower on top of the sub station building, and the police box on the left. (S Lockwood collection)

Old Toll Bar/Denaby

56.   Further along Doncaster Road, at the junction with Pastures Road, the former bears right over the Sheffield and South Yorkshire Navigation bridge, and then alongside the erstwhile Mexborough Power Station. Daimler 4 (originally 94) has crossed the bridge, and now passes the small Mexborough and Swinton Old Toll Bar depot on a return journey to Rotherham in March 1961. (J C Gillham)

57.   The railway level crossing in Doncaster Road, Denaby was a major cause of schedule disruption, but in this view the gates are open for Daimler 3 (originally 6) to cross in March 1961. The Denaby Main colliery is on the left, which is the current site of the Dearne Valley Leisure Centre. Automatic barriers now control the crossing, and the main road has been diverted to the right over a new bridge. This view has been taken from a footbridge over the railway, a site used frequently by enthusiast photographers. (J Copland/A D Packer copyright)

Conisbrough Low

58.   Vehicles continued along Doncaster Road past Station Road, where the Mexborough and Swinton service to Conisbrough High (Conanby) branched off, and into Low Road leading to the Brook Square terminus. In this view, Daimler 5 (originally 9) moves towards the terminus in March 1961, with the imposing Conisbrough Castle on the left; its fame was spread by Sir Walter Scott's novel "Ivanhoe". Rotherham trolleybuses never ran along the narrow roads around the castle that led to the Conisbrough High terminus, except on the last Sunday when Daimler 3 (originally 6) travelled the route with an enthusiasts' special. (J Copeland/A D Packer copyright)

59.   The turning circle at Brook Square had an extremely tight radius, which Mexborough and Swinton drivers negotiated with care, whilst the Rotherham three axle trolleybuses had difficulty, as will be seen from the next picture. In this view, Daimler 93 (later double deck 33) in as delivered livery, has been pulled tight to the wall of Mortimer's Dying and Cleaning works ready to complete the turn back. Note the ornate gas lamp and the lone Vauxhall saloon. (C Carter)

60.   Daimler 4 (originally 94) begins the tight turn back to Rotherham on full lock, with the conductor supervising, but still mounts the kerb. The buildings have been demolished and the road now leads to a major junction with the A630, which is controlled by traffic lights. Four brands of cigarette are advertised in the corner shop. (D S Giles/Omnibus Society copyright)

61.	Returning now to Rotherham, in later years the journey from the Mexborough and Swinton territory to the town centre and Frederick Street, was via a single line along Rawmarsh Road/Greasbrough Road from the Grafton Bridge. Daimler 6 (originally 10) makes the turn out of Greasbrough Road, before crossing Chantry Bridge over the River Don to reach the Frederick Street terminal stand. The Bridge Inn is on the right and the power station cooling tower again emphasises the industrial nature of the area. (J Fozard)

62.	Here we see Guy 43 (earlier 203, 13, 52 and later 65) crossing Chantry Bridge, and moving towards Frederick Street; the Bridge Inn is in the left background. Note the roof mounted resistors and the ornate gas lamp. The Greasbrough service would have used the bridge in both directions. (C Carter)

OUTWARDS TOWARDS KIMBERWORTH/TOLL BAR

This cross town service from Thrybergh opened on 17th May 1931. There was an extension to Toll Bar May 1948, which was cut back to Ewers Road in September 1953. Closure was on 2nd October 1965.

63.   Daimler 37 (originally single deck 17) has crossed town from Thrybergh, and having passed through Effingham Square, Frederick Street and Corporation Street, turns out of Westgate into Main Street on the journey out to Kimberworth. Ship Hill is on the right, and premises on the left include Fred Shaw's photographic business, and a Wimpy Bar. When the Templeborough service was in existence, vehicles would continue along Westgate to the rear of the photographer's position, before turning into Sheffield Road. (J Fozard)

Timetable 1963.

Fare Table 1963.

TROLLEY BUSES

SERVICE 6.—KIMBERWORTH (Ewers Road)
Via Main Street, Masbrough Street and Kimberworth Road

From CORPORATION STREET

Sunday			Monday to Friday			Saturday			
a.m.	p.m.	p.m.	a.m.	a.m.	p.m.	a.m.	a.m.	p.m.	p.m.
5.45	1.53	6.17	5.10	11.12	4.56	5.10	10.37	2.31	6.22
6.15	2.04	6.28	5.24	11.23	5.05	5.24	10.46	2.38	6.30
6.45	2.15	6.39	5.38	11.34	5.14	5.38	10.55	2.45	6.39
7.15	2.26	6.50	5.52	11.45	5.23	5.52	11.04	2.52	6.48
7.45	2.37	7.01	6.06	11.56	5.32	6.06	11.13	2.59	6.57
9.18	2.48	7.12	6.20	p.m.	5.41	6.20	11.22	3.06	7.06
9.36	2.59	7.23	6.34	12.07	5.50	6.34	11.29	3.13	7.15
9.54	3.10	7.34	6.43	12.18	5.59	6.43	11.36	3.20	7.24
10.12	3.21	7.45	6.52	12.29	6.10	6.52	11.43	3.27	7.33
10.30	3.32	7.56	7.01	12.40	6.21	7.01	11.50	3.34	7.42
10.48	3.43	8.07	7.10	12.51	6.32	7.10	11.57	3.41	7.51
11.06	3.54	8.18	7.19	1.02	6.43	7.19	p.m.	3.48	8.00
11.24	4.05	8.29	7.28	1.13	6.54	7.28	12.04	3.55	8.09
11.42	4.16	8.40	7.37	1.24	7.05	7.37	12.11	4.02	8.18
12.00	4.27	8.51	7.46	1.35	7.16	7.46	12.18	4.09	8.27
p.m.	4.38	9.02	7.55	1.46	7.27	7.55	12.25	4.16	8.36
12.18	4.49	9.13	8.04	1.57	7.38	8.04	12.32	4.23	8.45
12.36	5.00	9.24	8.13	2.08	7.49	8.13	12.39	4.30	8.54
12.47	5.11	9.35	8.22	2.19	8.00	8.22	12.46	4.37	9.03
12.58	5.22	9.46	8.31	2.30	8.11	8.31	12.53	4.44	9.12
1.09	5.33	10.00	8.40	2.41	8.22	8.40	1.00	4.51	9.21
1.20	5.44	10.10	8.49	2.52	8.33	8.49	1.07	4.58	9.30
1.31	5.55	10.19	9.00	3.03	8.44	8.58	1.14	5.05	9.39
1.42	6.06	10.30	9.11	3.14	8.55	9.07	1.21	5.12	9.48
		10.45	9.22	3.25	9.06	9.16	1.28	5.19	9.57
			9.33	3.36	9.17	9.25	1.35	5.26	10.06
			9.44	3.44	9.28	9.34	1.42	5.33	10.15
			9.55	3.53	9.39	9.43	1.49	5.40	10.24
			10.06	4.02	9.50	9.52	1.56	5.47	10.35
			10.17	4.11	10.01	10.01	2.03	5.54	10.45
			10.28	4.20	10.12	10.10	2.10	6.01	
			10.39	4.29	10.23	10.19	2.17	6.08	
			10.50	4.38	10.34	10.28	2.24	6.15	
			11.01	4.47	10.45				

Service No. 6—Kimberworth (Ewers Road)

Stage		
*1		Rotherham (Corporation Street) (1)
2	2½	Millmoor or Ferham Road (bottom) (2)
*3	3	2½ Ewers Road (3)

64.   Having left Main Street, Daimler 42 (originally single deck 14), has travelled along Masbrough Street in the background, and is about to crest Coronation Bridge outward to Kimberworth. The railways underneath comprise an avoiding line leaving the track from Sheffield to Rotherham Central station at Holmes, plus the route from North Derbyshire. On the right, at the foot of the bridge, is the erstwhile Rotherham United Millmoor football ground, which has been replaced by the New York Stadium. (R F Mack)

65.   On the opposite side of the bridge, Daimler 43 (originally single deck 16) completes the descent to the junction with Ferham Road on the right, which leads to the A6109 to Sheffield. A short working turning circle was provided at this point, particularly for football specials when Rotherham United were playing at home. The overhead wiring for the turning circle can be seen in this view; Mexborough and Swinton vehicles also used the facility on match days. The hoardings include advertisements for Persil and Rolo, brands that have stood the test of time. (R Brook/P Watson copyright)

66.   Daimler 31 (originally single deck 15) climbs Kimberworth Road, on the last section of the journey from Thrybergh; the location is between Cross Street and Charnwood Grove. The large house behind the parked Austin van still stands, but is obscured by the front garden trees. (V Nutton/Travel Lens Photographic)

➔ 67. Having left the Ewers Road, Kimberworth terminus a little further back, Daimler 39 (originally single deck 82) rounds the bend in Kimberworth Road, with the current Community Primary School on the left. It will shortly descend the incline seen in the previous picture. (V Nutton/Travel Lens Photographic)

➔ 68. Daimler 26 (originally single deck 85) waits at the Ewers Road terminus, with the destination blind set to indicate the cross town service back to Thrybergh. The original service that opened in May 1931, continued further along Church Street and High Street to the Colin Campbell public house. It was further extended to Toll Bar in May 1948, and a short working facility retained at Ewers Road. The service was cut back to this latter point in September 1953, by which time the turning circle illustrated had been constructed to replace the original reverser. Note the contact skate on the positive wire above 26, a feature that also appeared at other Rotherham termini. Before electric street illumination became common, sparse gas lighting sufficed, which gave little aid to trolleybus drivers when turning round, particularly in foggy weather. The contact skates were used to switch on/off additional lighting to help drivers, but fell out of use as general street lighting improved. (R L Wilson/OTA)

69.　　The original Colin Campbell, Kimberworth turning circle was at the road junction to the immediate left. The hostelry is now known as "The Colin". Daimler, probably 76 (later 7), enters High Street on a return journey towards Rotherham, with Old Wortley Road leading up the hill towards the Toll Bar terminus. Note the semi rural nature of the area, and the lack of other traffic. (F Tompkin)

70.　　Daimler 10 (later 6) waits at the Toll Bar terminus, with the turning circle wiring in the background, at the junction with Upper Wortley Road; Old Wortley Road is to the rear of the photographer's position. This post war extension includes a number of rigid wooden spaced twin line hangers, which can be seen in the upper foreground. (S L Smith/P Fox copyright)

OUTWARDS TOWARDS THRYBERGH

This cross town service from Kimberworth opened on 17th May 1931. Extensions were to Silverwood Colliery, and along Mowbray Street/Herringthorpe Valley Road. Closure was on 2nd October 1965.

Pumping Station

71.   The vehicles serving Pumping Station, Silverwood Colliery and Thrybergh shared common wiring for the first part of their journey along Fitzwilliam Road from the town centre. The Pumping Station service layover in the town centre was in All Saints Square, and subsequently Corporation Street. Daimler 93 (later double deck 33) waits at the end of Fitzwilliam Road in June 1955, before departing to the town centre, and onward to Kimberworth. Whilst in the early days Pumping Station vehicles turned here, a later extension in 1933 along Herringthorpe Valley Road and Mowbray Street, the latter in the background behind the lorry at the traffic island, provided a single line turning facility from either direction. Later, in 1939, a turning circle was provided at the end of Mowbray Street, thereby creating two way traffic from/to the main road. The overhead turnout junction, which has been set back on the approach from Rotherham, can be seen in the middle foreground, and all the property on the right has disappeared. (J Copland/A D Packer copyright)

Newspaper cutting 5th May 1956

72.   Daimler 37 (originally single deck 17) begins the turn into Mowbray Street in October 1965, using the inside overhead wiring, whilst that on the outside continued along Doncaster Road towards Thrybergh. Note the curved segment twin line hangers in the wiring, and the overhead turnout junction seen in the previous picture in the distance. The original Pumping Station was in the area to the rear of the trolleybus. (J Copland/A D Packer copyright)

73.   Here we see Daimler 27 (originally single deck 81) leaving Mowbray Street to join the main route back to Rotherham, which is to the rear of the photographer's position. A Ferguson tractor waits for the trolleybus to pass. The shop on the corner is now a ladies' hairdressers. (C Carter)

TROLLEY BUSES
SERVICE 5.—PUMPING STATION
Via Frederick Street, Fitzwilliam Road and Mowbray Street

From CORPORATION STREET.

Sunday		Monday to Friday			Saturday			
a.m.	p.m.	a.m.	a.m.	p.m.	a.m.	a.m.	p.m.	p.m.
5.00	4.33	4.36	9.50	4.48	4.36	9.24	1.48	6.24
5.24	4.55	5.00	10.12	5.00	5.00	9.36	2.00	6.36
5.48	5.17	5.12	10.34	5.12	5.12	9.48	2.12	6.48
7.36	5.39	5.24	10.56	5.24	5.24	10.00	2.24	7.00
p.m.	6.01	5.36	11.18	5.36	5.36	10.12	2.36	7.12
12.31	6.23	5.48	11.40	5.48	5.48	10.24	2.48	7.24
12.53	6.45	6.00	p.m.	6.00	6.00	10.36	3.00	7.36
1.15	7.07	6.12	12.02	6.16	6.12	10.48	3.12	7.48
1.37	7.29	6.24	12.24	6.38	6.24	11.00	3.24	8.00
1.59	7.51	6.36	12.46	7.00	6.36	11.12	3.36	8.12
2.21	8.13	6.48	1.08	7.22	6.48	11.24	3.48	8.24
2.43	8.35	7.00	1.30	7.44	7.00	11.36	4.00	8.36
3.05	9.08	7.12	1.52	8.06	7.12	11.48	4.12	8.48
3.27	9.30	7.24	2.14	8.28	7.24	12.00	4.24	9.00
3.49	9.52	7.36	2.36	8.50	7.36	p.m.	4.36	9.12
4.11	10.14	7.48	2.58	9.12	7.48	12.12	4.48	9.24
	10.40	8.00	3.20	9.34	8.00	12.24	5.00	9.36
		8.12	3.36	9.56	8.12	12.36	5.12	9.48
		8.24	3.48	10.18	8.24	12.48	5.24	10.00
		8.36	4.00	10.43	8.36	1.00	5.36	10.11
		8.48	4.12		8.48	1.12	5.48	10.22
		9.06	4.24		9.00	1.24	6.00	10.33
		9.28	4.36		9.12	1.36	6.12	10.44

From PUMPING STATION

Sunday		Monday to Friday			Saturday			
a.m.	p.m.	a.m.	a.m.	p.m.	a.m.	a.m.	p.m.	p.m.
5.12	4.44	4.48	9.39	4.36	4.48	9.36	2.00	6.36
5.36	5.06	5.12	10.01	4.48	5.12	9.48	2.12	6.48
6.00	5.28	5.24	10.23	5.00	5.24	10.00	2.24	7.00
7.48	5.50	5.36	10.45	5.12	5.36	10.12	2.36	7.12
p.m.	6.12	5.48	11.07	5.24	5.48	10.24	2.48	7.24
12.42	6.34	6.00	11.29	5.36	6.00	10.36	3.00	7.36
1.04	6.56	6.12	11.51	5.48	6.12	10.48	3.12	7.48
1.26	7.18	6.24	p.m.	6.00	6.24	11.00	3.24	8.00
1.48	7.40	6.36	12.13	6.12	6.36	11.12	3.36	8.12
2.10	8.02	6.48	12.35	6.27	6.48	11.24	4.00	8.24
2.32	8.24	7.00	12.57	6.49	7.00	11.36	4.00	8.36
2.54	8.46	7.12	1.19	7.11	7.12	11.48	4.12	8.48
3.16	9.19	7.24	1.41	7.33	7.24	12.00	4.24	9.00
3.38	9.41	7.36	2.03	7.55	7.36	p.m.	4.36	9.12
4.00	10.03	7.48	2.25	8.17	7.48	12.12	4.48	9.24
4.22	10.25	8.00	2.47	8.39	8.00	12.24	5.00	9.36
	10.51	8.12	3.09	9.01	8.12	12.36	5.12	9.48
		8.24	3.31	9.23	8.24	12.48	5.24	10.00
		8.36	3.48	9.45	8.36	1.00	5.36	10.11
		8.48	4.00	10.07	8.48	1.12	5.48	10.22
		9.00	4.12	10.29	9.00	1.24	6.00	10.33
		9.17	4.24	10.54	9.12	1.36	6.12	10.44
					9.24	1.48	6.24	10.55

74.   Daimler 37 (originally single deck 17) makes its way along Mowbray Street on a return trip from the Pumping Station terminus, under 18ins (457 mm) spaced overhead with mixed design twin line hangers. To the left are prefabricated bungalows (prefabs), which were built after the Second World War to overcome housing shortages. As indicated earlier, after withdrawal this vehicle passed through a number of enthusiast group owners, and is now in the hands of the Rotherham 37 Group, where it operates at the Trolleybus Museum, Sandtoft, North Lincolnshire. (V Nutton/Travel Lens Photographic)

Timetable 1963

75.	The conductor takes a breather as Daimler 38 (originally single deck 80) waits at the Pumping Station turning circle. Herringthorpe Valley Road is in the background, where there was a single line connection along this thoroughfare back to Doncaster Road.
(J Copland/A D Packer copyright)

→	76. Daimler 6 (originally 10), the last active single decker, makes its way along Herringthorpe Valley Road, under the single set of overhead wiring, back towards Doncaster Road. This wiring allowed short workings between the Pumping Station and Silverwood colliery.
(A B Cross)

→	77. Daimler 39 (originally single deck 82) leaves Doncaster Road, and approaches the traffic island at the junction with Mowbray Street on a return trip to Kimberworth from Thrybergh. The overhead wiring leading to the right allowed vehicles from Silverwood colliery to return there at shift changes via Mowbray Street and Herringthorpe Valley Road. The building in the centre is all that remains of the erstwhile Pumping Station, and the Series 2 Morris Minor, and Ford Zephyr Mk 2 complete the picture. (V Nutton/Travel Lens Photographic)

78. An immaculate Daimler 31 (originally single deck 15) has just left the Mowbray Street junction, and will continue along Doncaster Road towards Old Gate Lane, and onwards to Thrybergh. In the background is the Foljamble Arms Hotel, which has been demolished to make way for apartment blocks. (J Fozard)

Fare Table 1963

Service Nos. 5 and 6—Pumping Station and Thrybergh (Park Lane)

Stage							
*1	Rotherham (Corporation Street) (1)						
2	2½	Shakespeare Road (2)					
3	3	2½	School Street (3)				
**4	3	2½	2½	Pumping Station (4)			
5	4	3	2½	2½	Dalton Lane (5)		
6	4½	4	2½	2½	2½	Grapes Hotel (6)	
*7	5	4½	4	4	2½	2½	Park Lane (7)

For Children's Fares see Page 6

Special Fares—

Rotherham to Whinney Hill (Bottom) ... ... 4½d.
Pumping Station ,, ,, ,, ... 2½d.

79.   Daimler 30 (originally single deck 79) breasts the summit of Old Gate Lane, before descending down to the Doncaster Road junction. On the right is the Thrybergh British Legion Club, now a Sports and Social Club, selling Barnsley Bitter from the Oakwell Brewery, plus a very low-slung perambulator. (J Copland)

80.   A little further on, Daimler 29 (originally single deck 75) passes St Peters Church on Old Gate Lane, shortly before reaching the Park Lane/Hollings Lane junction, and will travel along the former to reach the Thrybergh terminus at Vale Road. (V Nutton/Travel Lens Photographic)

81.   At the top of Old Gate Lane, Dalton, Daimler 36 (originally single deck 92) rounds the curve into Park Lane outward from the town centre to Thrybergh in October 1965. The car on the right is an Austin 105 Westminster. (R D H Symons)

82.   Having left the Thrybergh terminus, and travelled along Park Lane, and then over the railway bridge in the background, Daimler 40 (originally single deck 8) is about to pass the Hollings Lane Post Office, with the named thoroughfare off to the right. This is where the Silverwood Colliery service left the main road and travelled along Hollings Lane to reach the pit complex; this will be covered in the next section. The post office is advertising a variety of cigarette brands, plus the ever popular Tizer drink. (C Carter)

TROLLEY BUSES

SERVICE 6.—THRYBERGH (Park Lane)

Via Frederick Street, Fitzwilliam Road, Doncaster Road, Oldgate Lane
and Park Lane

From CORPORATION STREET.

Sunday			Monday to Friday			Saturday			
a.m.	p.m.	p.m.	a.m.	a.m.	p.m.	a.m.	a.m.	p.m.	p.m.
5.10	1.31	6.17	5.04	11.12	5.00	5.04	10.41	2.32	6.25
5.50	1.42	6.28	5.18	11.23	5.09	5.18	10.50	2.39	6.34
6.15	1.53	6.39	5.32	11.34	5.18	5.32	10.59	2.46	6.43
6.45	2.04	6.50	5.46	11.45	5.27	5.46	11.08	2.53	6.52
7.00	2.15	7.01	6.00	11.56	5.36	6.00	11.17	3.00	7.01
7.15	2.26	7.12	6.14	p.m.	5.45	6.14	11.26	3.07	7.10
7.30	2.37	7.23	6.28	12.07	5.54	6.28	11.30	3.14	7.19
7.45	2.48	7.34	6.42	12.18	6.03	6.42	11.37	3.21	7.28
9.22	2.59	7.45	6.56	12.29	6.12	6.56	11.44	3.28	7.37
9.40	3.10	7.56	7.05	12.40	6.21	7.05	11.51	3.35	7.46
9.58	3.21	8.07	7.14	12.51	6.32	7.14	11.58	3.42	7.55
10.16	3.32	8.18	7.23	1.02	6.43	7.23	p.m.	3.49	8.04
10.34	3.43	8.29	7.32	1.13	6.54	7.32	12.05	3.56	8.13
10.52	3.54	8.40	7.41	1.24	7.05	7.41	12.12	4.03	8.22
11.10	4.05	8.51	7.50	1.35	7.16	7.50	12.19	4.10	8.31
11.28	4.16	9.02	7.59	1.46	7.27	7.59	12.26	4.17	8.40
11.46	4.27	9.13	8.08	1.57	7.38	8.08	12.33	4.24	8.49
p.m.	4.38	9.24	8.17	2.08	7.49	8.17	12.40	4.31	8.58
12.04	4.49	9.35	8.26	2.19	8.00	8.26	12.47	4.38	9.07
12.22	5.00	9.46	8.35	2.30	8.11	8.35	12.54	4.45	9.16
12.36	5.11	9.57	8.44	2.41	8.22	8.44	1.01	4.52	9.25
12.47	5.22	10.08	8.53	2.52	8.33	8.53	1.08	4.59	9.34
12.58	5.33	10.24	9.01	3.03	8.44	9.02	1.15	5.06	9.43
1.09	5.44	10.35	9.11	3.14	8.55	9.11	1.22	5.13	9.52
1.20	5.55	10.45	9.22	3.25	9.06	9.20	1.29	5.20	10.01
	6.06		9.33	3.36	9.17	9.29	1.36	5.27	10.10
			9.44	3.47	9.28	9.38	1.43	5.34	10.19
			9.55	3.57	9.39	9.47	1.50	5.41	10.28
			10.06	4.06	9.50	9.56	1.57	5.48	10.37
			10.17	4.15	10.01	10.05	2.04	5.55	10.45
			10.28	4.24	10.12	10.14	2.11	6.02	
			10.39	4.33	10.23	10.23	2.18	6.09	
			10.50	4.42	10.34	10.32	2.25	6.16	
			11.01	4.51	10.45				

83. At the lower end of Park Lane, Daimler 30 (originally single deck 79) crosses the bridge seen in the previous picture on its way back to the town centre and Kimberworth, with a second trolleybus in the far distance. The railway line beneath the bridge led from Thrybergh Junction towards the Silverwood sidings to the right. The slippered young lady on the left appears to be returning home with an armful of fish and chips.
(V Nutton/Travel Lens Photographic)

Timetable 1963

84.   Daimler 32 (originally single deck 12) waits at the Thrybergh terminus; the sweep of the turning circle wiring is mirrored by the wheel scrubbing on the road surface immediately below. Vale Road is on the right and curves round to meet the Silverwood route in Hollings Lane. The current Thrybergh School and Sports College is in the right background, and the ornate gas lamp in the foreground completes the picture. (J Fozard)

85.   Daimler 32 (originally single deck 12) rounds the bend in Hollings Lane before joining Old Gate Lane at the previously mentioned post office, and then onwards to the town centre or Pumping Station. It is on a return journey from Silverwood Colliery, where services operated to match colliery shift changes. Note the open countryside towards Dalton Magna and Wickersley. This colliery service commenced on 2nd June 1931. (V Nutton/Travel Lens Photographic)

86.   Having rounded the bend at the junction of Hollings Lane and Vale Road, Daimler 32 puts in another appearance, and begins the short rise to Round Wood on an outwards trip to the colliery. From here, Vale Road curves round through a housing estate to join Park Lane at the terminus of the Thrybergh service. (V Nutton/Travel Lens Photographic)

87.　On a stretch of road between the two previous pictures, Daimler 33 (originally single deck 93) returns from the colliery, with only one other vehicle in sight. The overhead wiring has 18ins (457mm) spacing rather than the more normal 24ins (610mm), and bracket arm suspension was used on long stretches of this route. The telegraph poles are a feature not seen in today's road scene. (V Nutton/Travel Lens Photographic)

Timetable
1963

TROLLEY BUSES
SERVICE 49.—SILVERWOOD COLLIERY

Via Corporation Street, Frederick Street, Fitzwilliam Road,
Doncaster Road, Dalton and Oldgate Lane.

From CORPORATION STREET

SUNDAY		MONDAY TO FRIDAY				SATURDA
a.m.	p.m.	a.m.	a.m.	p.m.	p.m.	a.m.	a.r
4.40	12.13	3.50	7.50	12.33	5.33	3.50	11.1
5.00	1.10	4.30	8.25	12.50	7.10	4.30	11.1
5.15	1.30	4.35	9.30ʀ	12.55	7.30	4.40	p.r
5.30	8.45	4.40	9.50ʀ	1.00	7.40	5.20	12.
6.20	9.00	4.50	10.10ʀ	1.05ʀ	8.15	5.40	12.:
8.00	9.20	5.00	10.30ʀ	1.15	8.55	5.50	12.
	9.40	5.10	10.48ʀ	1.33	9.05	6.15	1.
		ʀ5.10	11.00	1.40	9.15	7.10	1.
		5.20	11.15	1.55	9.30	11.10	
		5.30	11.30ʀ	2.15	10.23		
		ʀ5.30	11.45ʀ	3.00			
		5.40	p.m.	3.25			
		6.15	12.05	3.40			
		7.10	12.15	4.50			

From SILVERWOOD COLLIERY

SUNDAY		MONDAY TO FRIDAY				SATURDA
a.m.	p.m.	a.m.	a.m.	p.m.	p.m.	a.m.	a.
4.55	1.35	4.10	8.45	12.55	6.00	4.10	11.
5.30	1.55	x4.50	9.50ʀ	1.15	7.40	5.00	p.
6.05	9.03	5.00	10.10ʀ	1.35	7.55	5.20	12
6.40	9.17	5.10	10.30ʀ	1.45	8.37	5.45	12
8.15	9.40	5.20	10.50ʀ	1.55	8.55	6.05	12
p.m.	10.03	5.40	11.10ʀ	2.05	9.10	6.45	1
12.32		5.55	11.40	2.20	9.35	7.30	1
		6.10	11.57ʀ	2.55	10.05	11.35	1
		6.40	p.m.	3.20	10.50		
		6.50	12.15ʀ	3.45			
		7.33	12.30	4.10			
		8.07	12.40	5.15			

ʀ—Starts from Pumping Station.
x—To Pumping Station only.
ʀ—Fridays only.

Subject to alteration or cancellation according to Colliery requirements.

For further journeys to and from Silverwood Colliery, see
Services 22 and 49 (Motor Buses) Time Tables

Fare Table 1963

Service No. 49.—Silverwood Colliery (Trolley Buses)

Stage									
*1							Rotherham (Effingham Square or All Saints' Square) (1)		
2	2½						Shakespeare Road (2)		
3	3	2½					School Street (3)		
4	3	2½	2½				Pumping Station (4)		
5	4	3	2½	2½			Dalton Lane (5)		
6	4½	4	2½	2½	2½		Grapes Hotel (6)		
7	5	4½	4	4	2½	2½	Thrybergh W.M. Club (7)		
*8	6	6	4½	4½	4	4	3	Silverwood Colliery (8)	

For Children's Fares see Page 6

Special Fares—

Between	Pumping Station and Whinney Hill (bottom)	...	...	...	...	2½d.
,,	Junction of Hollings Lane/Vale Road and Silverwood	...	...	...	2½d.
,,	Cross Street and Silverwood	...	...	...	...	3d.
,,	Rotherham and Whinney Hill (bottom)	...	...	...	...	4½d.

88.   At a shift change, Daimler 20 waits outside the colliery in April 1954 ready for the return to Rotherham, having turned at the circle in the distance. This vehicle was one of those that saw further service in Cadiz, Spain. The road continues onwards to Braithwell. (J Copland/A D Packer copyright)

89.   Also in April 1954, Daimler 91 (later double deck 34) moves out of the Silverwood turning circle, with the colliery buildings and electrical distribution equipment in the background. Although most return journeys ran through to Rotherham, some only travelled as far as Pumping Station to cater for miners that lived in the area. (J Copland/A D Packer copyright)

GREASBROUGH

This service opened on 7th July 1936 and closed on 27th May 1951.

90.   This far from clear view has been included as it depicts the short working facility on the Greasbrough service. It comprised a "round the houses" circuit of Cross Street, Providence Street and Firth Street, which under the earlier numbering system was Service 33, designated Munsbrough Lane, depicted on the left. In this view, the overhead wiring out of Firth Street can be seen with an unidentified Daimler descending Potter Hill. The Greasbrough parish church of St Marys can be seen in the distance, which the vehicle depicted will pass to reach the terminus. The small boy next to the right hand bus stop is the photographer's son. (C C Hall)

➔   91. The Greasbrough terminus was round a rectangular open area at Green Street. Here Daimler 88, also eventually destined for Spain, is seen leaving Main Street, and entering the first leg of the rectangular turn. Having travelled around the open area, it will then re-enter Main Street for the return to the town centre. The return overhead wiring can be seen in the background.
(R Marshall/Omnibus Society collection)

➔   92. Daimler 86, which subsequently operated in Spain, waits outside the Greasbrough Brass Band Club and Institute, now a Working Men's Club, before returning to the town centre, having just left the terminal loop. (R Marshall/Omnibus Society collection)

TEMPLEBOROUGH

This wartime extension was opened in March 1940 and wiring removed by the end of 1949.

93.   Following the outbreak of the 1939-1945 War, the joint tram service to Sheffield was wired for trolleybuses as far as Templeborough. This allowed services from the Rotherham outer termini, and Kilnhurst Road, Rawmarsh, to the various steel works in the Templeborough area that were concentrating on production for the war effort. In this post war view, Ransomes 22 (originally 26 and previously 37) will pass under a section insulator/feeder, before completing the turn back to Bramley via the town centre. Bramley was the last short working facility before Maltby, and at the time was allocated service number 22. With the closure of the tramway system, the trolleybus overhead wiring was removed by the end of 1949. To allow vehicles from the Maltby direction to enter All Saints Square for this wartime service, wiring

was erected round Davy's Corner from College Street. Vehicles would then circle round Upper Millgate, Corporation Street, Frederick Street and Howard Street into Effingham Street, and thence to College Street and High Street. On return from Templeborough, vehicles would enter Corporation Street and complete a partial circuit round to College Street, before slipping across to the outward Maltby wiring. Note the single end Rotherham tram Car 8. (R Brook)

↑ 94. Rotherham's single ended trams, purchased in 1934/35, were used on the joint service to Sheffield, made possible by turning loops at each end. Earlier, Sheffield had not agreed to introduce trolleybuses on the joint service, and these Rotherham trams continued to Templeborough until 1949, the joint service to Sheffield having ceased the previous year. Here Car 9, on a short working to Templeborough, is about to use the reverser at Temple Street, much as a trolleybus would on a similar configured turning facility. However, here trolleybuses returning to Rotherham used a conventional turning circle, the wiring for which can be seen to the right of the tram upper deck. (G Hearse/ Travel Lens Photographic)

DEPOT AND APPROACHES

95. The depot forecourt in June 1948, with Car 14 at the Rawmarsh Road entrance, and a second car behind. 14 was originally Leeds 125 (125A from 1927) dating from 1908, hired by Rotherham in 1943, and eventually purchased in 1948, now with the top deck open balcony enclosed. One of the Sunbeam trolleybuses in the 70-77 series can also be seen. (R B Parr)

96.   Mexborough and Swinton Sunbeam 29 approaches the start of the town terminal loop, with the Rotherham depot in the background. It is on a return trip on the joint service from Conisbrough Low, and will continue along Rawmarsh Road towards the Bridge Inn and Chantry Bridge on the first leg of the loop. The car on the left is a Morris Series Six MS saloon. (R H G Simpson)

97.   Daimler 35 (originally single deck 78) turns out of Rawmarsh Road onto Graffton Bridge, having left the depot in the background. This nearside overhead wiring provided egress from the depot to Effingham Street, and the town centre stands. The adjacent wiring across the bridge provided access to the depot and onwards to the Mexborough and Swinton territory to the north. The wiring leaving the picture top left was the beginning of the terminal loop along the continuation of Rawmarsh Road referred to earlier. (D F Parker)

98.　　Inside the depot, Daimler 25 (originally single deck 83) heads a line of similar vehicles, and appears to have made a return journey from Thrybergh or Kimberworth. The overhead wiring is mounted in troughing suspended from the roof trusses. (D F Parker)

ROLLING STOCK

99.	1912	38 - 40	**Initially no registration**	**Railless Electric Traction (RET)**
			ET 1922 - 1924 (1921)	
		T1 - T3	**Renumbered** (1916)	
		T1 to 51	**Renumbered** (1926)	
	1913	41 - 43	**Initially no registration**	**Railless Electric Traction (RET)**
		T4 - T6	**Renumbered** (1916)	
		T4	**ET 1925** (1921)	

These were the first six vehicles acquired for the Maltby service, and had 26 seat (also reported as 25 and 28 seats) rear entrance bodies by Milnes Voss, although there are also suggestions that those for 42/43 were by Lockwood and Hobson (or Clarkson). David Brown provided the chassis, and the electrical equipment and motors were by Siemens. T1 (38) was modified to front entrance in 1923 to allow for one man operation; all were withdrawn by 1928. 39 is depicted on display in Haymarket, adjacent to Fitzalan Square, Sheffield on 20th October 1912. Power is being taken from the single positive tram overhead wire, with the negative return via the front axle two-wheeled attachment running in the tram track. (Omnibus Society collection)

	1921	T5 - T6	**ET 1926 - 1927**	**Railless Limited**	(No photograph)
		55 - 56	**Renumbered**	**(c 1926)**	

These two vehicles appear to have replaced the earlier T5 and T6, and had 32 seat front entrance bodies by the Corporation; they were modified later to central entrance and were withdrawn in 1931. There is a doubt whether these were new vehicles, but perhaps rebodied from two of the original six trolleybuses.

100.	1922	T2	ET 2337	Straker – Clough	
		52	Renumbered	(c 1926)	
	1924	T3 - T4	ET 2840 - 2841	Straker – Clough	
		53 - 54	Renumbered	(c 1926)	
		18 / 41	Renumbered	(1933)	

The next three vehicles had BTH motors and Roe 26 seat front entrance bodies, which were later modified to central entrance with 32 seats. Pneumatic tyres were fitted in 1926, and withdrawal came in 1932/33. This view shows 52 in the depot yard, incorporating the above changes. Until the mid 1930s, the trolleybuses were known as Railless Electric Vehicles (REVs) by the management, with members of the public referring to them as "trackless" until the end. (Omnibus Society collection)

101. **1925 T7 - T8   ET 3340 - 3341 Straker - Clough**
        57 - 58   Renumbered   (c 1926)
        58 to 45   Renumbered   (c 1928)
        45 to 42   Renumbered   (1929)
        57 to 17   Renumbered   (c 1933)

These two vehicles were similar to T2 – T4 above, with a 32 seat front entrance body by Roe, and were subjected to all the same modifications. 17 was used as an illuminated trolleybus from 1935 to the 1940s, and withdrawn in 1945. The other vehicle was withdrawn in 1935. T8 is depicted when new outside the bodybuilder's premises. (Omnibus Society collection)

102. **1927   50/47 - 49 ET 3217/4818 - 4820 Straker - Clough**

This delivery was again similar to earlier batches, although delivered with Roe central entrance bodies. The registration of 50 was originally booked in 1924, but not used until later. 47 - 49 were the last trolleybuses produced by the manufacturer. The whole batch were sold to Darlington Corporation in 1936, becoming their 46/47/45/44, and were a short term expedient pending the delivery of new Leyland trolleybuses in 1937. Withdrawal came in 1938, and they were stored until the early days of the 1939 -1945 War. 49 is seen outside the bodybuilder's factory. (G Lumb collection)

103.	1928	46	Guy BTX (3-axle) ET 4933
		45	Renumbered (1939)
	1929	43-45	Guy BTX (3-axle) ET 5284 - 5286
		45 to 44	Renumbered (1939)

For the joint services operated with the Mexborough and Swinton company to the north of the town, four 3-axle vehicles were purchased. They had Roe 32 seat central entrance bodies, and Rees Roturbo motors. Vehicles were withdrawn between 1939 and the early 1940s. There were slight bodywork differences between the two deliveries, and 44 is depicted in Effingham Street.
(W J Haynes/Omnibus Society collection)

| 104. | 1931 | 19-38 | Ransomes Sims → and Jefferies (2-axle) ET 6609 - 6628 |
| | | 39-40 | Ransomes Sims and Jefferies (2-axle) ET 6607 - 6608 |

There was substantial renumbering of these vehicles in the period 1933 to 1948, too numerous to be covered in this publication.

This large batch of vehicles had Ransomes motors, and 32 seat central entrance bodies by Cravens. They were used for the conversation of the Thrybergh and Kimberworth tram services, and the subsequent extension to Silverwood Colliery. Earliest withdrawals were in 1937, with two lasting until 1950. This official view depicts 30, which was withdrawn in 1945, and was one of the few in the batch not to be renumbered. (Omnibus Society collection)

| | 1930 | 51 | Guy BT (2-axle) ET 6020 | (No photograph) |
| | | 56 | Renumbered (1938) | |

This vehicle was a Guy demonstrator fitted with a Guy 32 seat central entrance body. It was eventually purchased and withdrawn in 1940.

105.   **1933**   **39 - 42   Guy BT 32 (2-axle)   ET 7885 - 7888**
                    52 - 54   Guy BT 32 (2-axle)   ET 7880 - 7882
                    57 - 59   Guy BT 32 (2-axle)   ET 7883/7884/7889
                    57 to 39   Renumbered (1939)
                    41/42/54 to 24 - 26   Renumbered (1947/48)

The bodywork for this batch of vehicles was split between Cravens (52 - 54/57/58), with Roberts building the remainder. All had 32 seat central entrances, and were fitted with Rees Roturbo motors. There were three pre-war withdrawals, with one vehicle lasting until 1950. 59 is seen in this official photograph when new, and prior to booms being fitted. The Roberts' bodies were fitted with luggage racks. (S Lockwood collection)

106. **1935 15 - 18 Guy BT 32 (2-axle)**
                     ET 9230 - 9233
      27 - 30   Renumbered (1947/48)
      59 - 62   Renumbered (1950)

Cravens secured the body order for these four vehicles, providing a central entrance and 32 seats. The motors were by ECC, and withdrawal came in 1951. 62 (final fleet number) stands in the depot forecourt. By this time, General Manager T P Sykes (1919-1943) had consolidated his specification for streamlined, single deck, central entrance trolleybuses for the municipality, from which he never wavered, thereby giving a reputation for providing speedy and comfortable public transport for the town.

(R Marshall/Omnibus Society collection)

107. **1936 60 - 65 Guy BTX (3-axle) →**
                     ET 9615 - 9620
      60 to 66   Renumbered (1940)
      61 - 66 to 31 - 36
                     Renumbered (1947/48)

A policy change resulted in all future vehicle orders specifying three-axle configuration. This increased the seating capacity to 40 (re-seated to 39 in 1945), whilst still retaining central entrances. Cravens were again the selected body supplier, and the motors were by ECC. East Lancashire Coachbuilders rebuilt 64 in 1945, and the batch was withdrawn in 1949/50. 33 (final fleet number) is seen here in Corporation Street destined for Kimberworth.

(R Marshall/Omnibus Society collection)

108.	1937/38	14/47 - 50/66/203	**Guy BTX**	**(3-axle)**	**AET 901 - 906/913**
		67 - 70/201/202/204	**AEC 664T**	**(3-axle)**	**AET 907 - 912/914**

There was substantial renumbering of these vehicles in the period 1938 to 1950,
too numerous to be covered in this publication.

A split chassis order was made for these deliveries. The Guys were fitted with the manufacturer's motors, whilst EEC units were used for the AECs. All had central entrance 39 seat bodies by Cravens, with seating reduced to 38 in 1947. 203 and 204 were exhibited at the 1937 Commercial Motor Show, and a number were rebuilt by East Lancashire Coachbuilders after the war. The batches were withdrawn between 1949 and 1954. Guy 203 poses in the depot yard with resistors mounted out of sight at the rear. These were later moved to the roof (see Picture 62). (R Marshall/Omnibus Society collection)

109.	1939	19 - 22	Guy BTX (3-axle)	CET 80 - 83
		55 - 58	Renumbered (1947/48)	
		56 - 58 to 69 - 71	Renumbered (1950)	
		23 - 26	AEC 664T (3-axle)	CET 84 - 87
		51 - 54	Renumbered (1947/48)	

A further split order from the two manufacturers, but this time fitted with East Lancashire Coachbuilders bodies with central entrances. The Guys had 38 seats and the AECs 39; the latter were reduced to 38 seats in 1946. Motors were again by Guy and EEC, and withdrawal occurred between 1950 and 1954. AEC 53 (final fleet number) is seen in Effingham Street awaiting a departure to Maltby.
(R Marshall/Omnibus Society collection)

110.	1940	70 - 77	**Sunbeam MS2C (3-axle) CET 480 - 487**
		59 - 66	**Renumbered (1947/48)**
		62 to 72	**Renumbered (1950)**
	1942	82 - 89	**Sunbeam MS2C (3-axle) CET 607 - 614**
		67 - 74	**Renumbered (1947/48)**
		67/73 to 73/74	**Renumbered (1950)**

These vehicles were fitted with GEC motors, and East Lancashire Coachbuilders 39 seat central entrance bodies; seating was reduced to 38 in 1945/46. Chassis failure in service resulted in all receiving strengthening modifications between 1944 and 1946. Perimeter seating was tried on 75, but returned to original format. Withdrawal started in 1949, and was completed in 1954. 73 (penultimate fleet number) awaits departure to Worry Goose Lane in Effingham Street, and is currently being restored by Tim Stubbs and members of the Rotherham Trolleybus Group. (See Pictures 13 and 117)
(R Marshall/Omnibus Society collection)

111.	1949	75 - 90	Daimler CT(E or C)6	(3-axle)	FET 335 – 350
	1950	91 - 94	Daimler CTE6	(3-axle)	FET 471 - 474
		1 - 24	Daimler CT(E or C)6	(3-axle)	FET 601 - 624

*There was substantial renumbering of these vehicles in the period 1956 to 1957,
too numerous to list in this publication.*

During the war, provisional orders were placed for eight AECs and thirty six Bristol trolleybuses, which eventually resulted in the forty four Daimler vehicles above. 75 - 83/85, 91 - 94 and 7 - 18 were fitted with EEC motors (suffix E), and the balance were from Crompton Parkinson (suffix C). All were fitted with East Lancashire Coachbuilders 38 seat central entrance bodies, with thirty six of the order having frames supplied from the main factory in Lancashire to East Lancashire (Bridlington) Ltd for completion. Twenty of the single deck trolleybuses were rebuilt to double deck format (and re numbered), with new 70 seat rear entrance bodies by Roe in 1956/57, which for a period improved the financial performance of the department. In 1960, seventeen surplus single deckers were sold to operators in Spain, fifteen going to Cadiz, and two to Lasarte, near San Sebastian. Both new owners reduced the seating, and converted them to dual entrance/exit, and in the case of Cadiz fitted their purchases with new bodies circa 1965. 22, in as delivered livery, waits in All Saints Square before making a return trip to Pumping Station. (R Marshall/Omnibus Society collection)

ROTHERHAM CORPORATION
S/DECK 3 AXLE TROLLEYBUS

Built: 1949/50 Daimler CTE 6	Scale:
Body: as built East Lancs.	4mm = 1 Foot
Fleet No. 1-24 & 75-94.	

DRAWING No. TB49

SCALE FEET 0 1 2 3 4 5 6 7 8 9 10 11 12

FET616, with others had English Electric electrical equipment, hence the CTE reference. Others in the batch were fitted with Crompton Parkinson equipment, hence the CTC reference.

VENTS AS LATER MODIFIED →
BUILT AS FULL WIDTH

VENTS AS BUILT

VENTS AS LATER MODIFIED

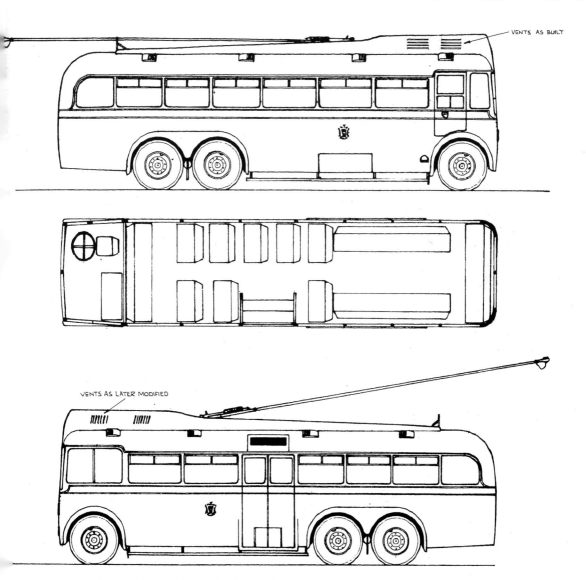

112.   Daimler 29 (originally single deck 75) illustrates the conversion to double deck format in 1956, as it waits at the Thrybergh terminus. The attractive lines of the Roe body are similar to those fitted to trolleybuses supplied to Huddersfield Corporation. The first fourteen had drop down V rain channels on the upper front corner pillars, whilst the remaining six had a continuous strip. These rebuilt vehicles were withdrawn between 1963, and the system closure in 1965. (R Marshall/Omnibus Society collection)

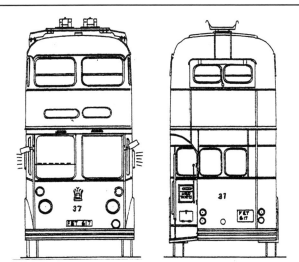

ROTHERHAM CORPORATION
D/DECK 3 AXLE TROLLEYBUS

Chassis: Daimler CTE 6	Scale:
Body: Roe 1956/57.	4mm = 1 Foot
Fleet No. 25-44.	

DRAWING No. TB67

SCALE
FEET   0 1 2 3 4 5 6 7 8 9 10 11 12

FET 617, with others had English Electric electrical equipment, hence the CTE reference. Others in the batch were fitted with Crompton Parkinson equipment, hence the CTC reference.

No. 25 – 38 were as drawn but on No. 39 – 44 the rain strip continued around the front above the windows with no drop-down vees at the top of the corner pillars.

Terry Russell. November 2006.

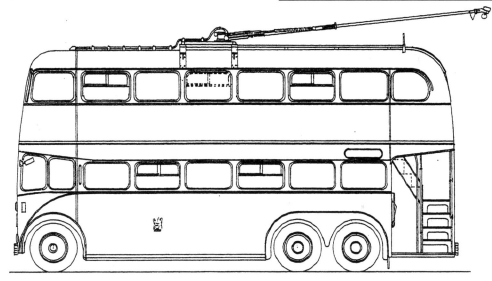

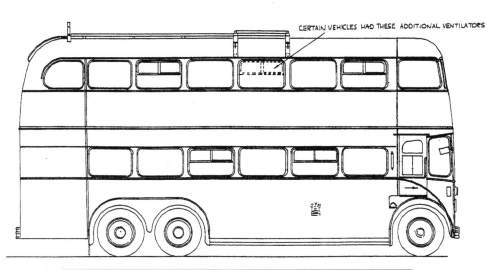

CERTAIN VEHICLES HAD THESE ADDITIONAL VENTILATORS

DRAWN BY: TERRY RUSSELL. 23, THORNDEN, COWFOLD, HORSHAM. WEST SUSSEX. RH13 8AG
FOR THE FULL LIST OF OVER 1000 DRAWINGS AND MODEL TRAM PARTS VISIT MY WEB SITE
www.terryrusselltrams.co.uk OR SEND 6 FIRST CLASS STAMPS FOR A PAPER COPY.

TOWER WAGON

113.   Tower Wagon 3 is assisting with the replacement of a traction standard in Corporation Street. This service vehicle was converted from a 1940 Bristol L5G single deck bus in 1956. When withdrawn in 1966, it was initially sold to the Maypine Trolleybus Company, which was a model trolleybus system operated in a Great Bookham garden. It was subsequently sold for spare parts. Four earlier tower wagons were used at various times between 1913 and 1943. Two post war vehicles on Bedford chassis, namely FET 195/196, purchased in 1949, lasted until 1965. The former has been restored, and resides at the South Yorkshire Transport Museum; FET 196 passed to the Teesside Railless Traction Board after closure of the Rotherham system. (J Fozard)

DONCASTER VISITOR

114.   Before the proposal to rebuild a number of single deck trolleybuses into double deck format was presented to the Transport Committee as a means of improving revenue, it was felt necessary to check the headroom under the Rotherham overhead wiring. Neighbouring Doncaster provided Karrier E6 362 on the 19th June 1955 to carry out the checks, with a tower wagon in close attendance. Geoff Warnes followed 362 from Doncaster to Rotherham on his bicycle in order to take a series of photographs of this unique event. This included an invitation from Rotherham's manager to take photographs in the depot yard, after realising an official record of the event was not in the day's schedule. Rotherham Daimler 80 (later double deck 38) passes the Doncaster vehicle, which is parked with booms down in Fitzwilliam Road. (G Warnes/Omnibus Society collection)

DECORATED VEHICLE

115.   Straker - Clough 17 (previously T7 and then 57) was converted into a decorated illuminated vehicle in 1935, and probably used to commemorate the coronation of King George IV in 1937; photographs also exist with the signage indicating "Happy New Year". The decorated vehicle is seen here in All Saints Square, and to the left is the rear of Bristol motorbus 88, which was new in 1932, and withdrawn by 1941. (S L Smith/P Fox copyright)

THE AFTER LIFE

117.   Three Rotherham trolleybuses survive in the United Kingdom. On the left is Daimler 37 (originally single deck 17), which has been restored, and is operational at the Trolleybus Museum at Sandtoft in North Lincolnshire. On the right is Sunbeam 73 (originally 88 and later 74), currently undergoing long term major restoration, mainly in Burton- on-Trent, but also at Sandtoft by Tim Stubbs and members of the Rotherham Trolleybus Group. East Lancashire Coachbuilders rebuilt the body in 1950, at which time the resistors were on the rear roof having originally been under the rear seating. During this rebuilding, the resistors were moved to the roof front, and covered by a streamline canopy, similar to that fitted to the bodies the company were building on the Daimler chassis. The restoration will result in the vehicle appearing in its pre 1950 condition (see Picture 10). In addition, a third vehicle, namely double deck Daimler 44 (originally single deck 18), is in store near Doncaster awaiting restoration (see Pictures 13 and 110). (T W Knowles)

116.   The Rotherham trolleybus system closed on Saturday 2nd October 1965, and the last service vehicle into the depot was Daimler 33 (originally single deck 93). The following day, two enthusiast tours took place, one organised by the Nottingham Trolleybus Group, travelling in Daimler 30 (originally single deck 79), and the other by the National Trolleybus Association, using Daimler 44 (originally single deck 18). In this view, 30 is seen outside the Rawmarsh Road depot, where an enterprising enthusiast (Dennis Vickers) has created an appropriate adornment; this was the very last trolleybus into the depot, and was subsequently scrapped; 44 is in store awaiting restoration. Thus ended 62 years of electrically powered public transport in the town, which included 53 years of trolleybus operation.
(R D H Symons)

118. As indicated earlier, the 1927 delivery of Straker - Clough vehicles were sold to Darlington Corporation in 1936. Withdrawal there came in 1938, after which they were stored until the early years of the 1939-1945 War. This obviously proved worthwhile, as this view shows one of the batch being used in what appears to be an Air Raid Precaution (ARP) exercise. (R Marshall collection)

➔ 119. Daimler 1 (originally 24) made the move to sunny Spain in 1960, together with Daimler 2 (originally 84), and became number 8 in the Tranvia de San Sebastian a Tolosa, Lasarte fleet. Both operated into San Sebastian from the inland towns of Lasarte and Tolosa, mainly on short workings from the former. While still retaining the original driving position, the single nearside entrance has been replaced by the dual entrance/ exit depicted, and seating reduced to 21. A front bumper bar, automatic boom retrievers and trailer towing gear were also fitted. Both were withdrawn in 1971; Daimler 2, which became 9 in the new owner's fleet, is thought to be undergoing restoration in Spain. (P Fox collection)

➔ 120. A sister vehicle is seen here operated by Tranvias de Cadiz a San Fernando; fifteen such vehicles were purchased via London shipping agent Gore Bruce in 1960, and exported to the Spanish operator. The side roof ventilation seems to have been removed, and automatic boom retrievers have been added, mounted below the rear windows. These vehicles were also converted to dual entrance/exit with seating reduced to 15, and were rebuilt with local bodies circa 1965. (P Fox collection)

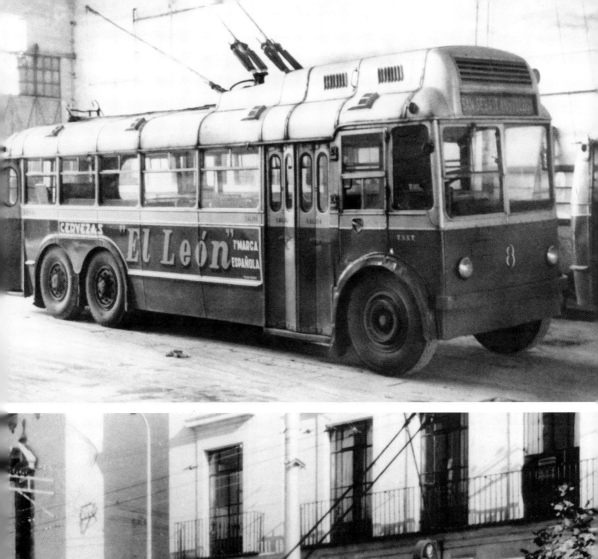

Middleton Press

Easebourne Lane, Midhurst, West Sussex.
GU29 9AZ   Tel:01730 813169
email:info@middletonpress.co.uk

ISBN PREFIXES - A-978 0 906520 B- 978 1 873793 C- 978 1 901706 D-978 1 904474 E - 978 1 906008 F - 978 1 908174

* BROCHURE AVAILABLE SHOWING RAILWAY ALBUMS AND NEW TITLES *
ORDER ONLINE - *PLEASE VISIT OUR WEBSITE* - www.middletonpress.co.uk